HARRAP'S

Croatian phrasebook

D0860749

McGraw·Hill

New York   Chicago   San Francisco   Lisbon   London   Madrid   Mexico City
Milan   New Delhi   San Juan   Seoul   Singapore   Sydney   Toronto

ISBN 0-07-148247-4

Editor & Project Manager
Anna Stevenson

Publishing Manager
Patrick White

Prepress
Isla MacLean
David Reid

CONTENTS

INTRODUCTION

This brand new English-Croatian phrasebook from Harrap is ideal for anyone wishing to try out their foreign language skills while travelling abroad. The information is practical and clearly presented, helping you to overcome the language barrier and mix with the locals.

Each section features a list of useful words and a selection of common phrases: some of these you will read or hear, while others will help you to express yourself. The simple phonetic transcription system, specifically designed for English speakers, ensures that you will always make yourself understood.

The book also includes a mini bilingual dictionary of around 4,500 words, so that more adventurous users can build on the basic structures and engage in more complex conversations.

Concise information on local culture and customs is provided, along with practical tips to save you time. After all, you're on holiday – time to relax and enjoy yourself! There is also a food and drink glossary to help you make sense of menus, and ensure that you don't miss out on any of the national or regional specialities.

Remember that any effort you make will be appreciated. So don't be shy – have a go!

PRONUNCIATION

A pronunciation guide has been provided for all Croatian words and phrases found in this book which you will need to express yourself. By simply reading the italic transliteration after each word or phrase you will be able to make yourself understood. Croatian pronunciation is not terribly difficult; every letter is pronounced. Remember that syllables in **bold** should be stressed.

letter	name of letter	pronunciation	transliteration
A a	ah	a as in f**a**ther	*a*
B b	be	b	*b*
C c	tse	ts as in ca**ts**	*ts*
Č č	che	ch as in **ch**urch	*ch*
Ć ć	che	roughly tj, as in cap**tu**re	*ch*
D d	de	d	*d*
DŽ dž	dze	j as in **j**et	*j*
Đ đ	dje	roughly dj, as in nee**d y**ou	*j*
E e	e	e as in b**e**d	*e*
F f	ef	f	*f*
G g	ge	g as in **g**one	*g*
H h	ha	**ch** as in lo**ch**	*H*
I i	ee	**e** as in h**e**	*ee*
J j	ye	**y** as in **y**es	*y*
K k	ka	k	*k*
L l	el	l	*l*
Lj lj	lyeu	**lli** as in mi**lli**on	*ly, l'*
M m	em	m	*m*
N n	en	n	*n*
Nj nj	nj	**n** as in **n**ews	*ny, n'*
O o	o	**o** as in n**o**t	*o*
P p	pe	p	*p*
R r	er	rolled r	*rr*
S s	es	**s** as in ble**ss**	*s*
Š š	sh	sh	*sh*
T t	te	t	*t*
U u	u	**ou** as in c**ou**ld	*oo*
V v	ve	v	*v*

letter	name of letter	pronunciation	transliteration
Z z	z	z	z
Ž ž	zh	**s** as in plea**s**ure	zh

Note that in this phrasebook the form given for adjectives and adverbs is the neuter, which may not always be appropriate for what you want to say. For the feminine and masculine forms, please consult the dictionary and the grammar sections.

ABBREVIATIONS USED IN THIS BOOK

acc	accusative	*m*	masculine
adj	adjective	*n*	neuter
adv	adverb	*nom*	nominative
dat	dative	*pl*	plural
f	feminine	*prep*	preposition
gen	genitive	*sg*	singular
inf	informal	*v*	verb
instr	instrumental	*voc*	vocative
loc	locative		

EVERYDAY CONVERSATION

Croats generally shake hands when they meet, or just nod. People generally only kiss each other on the cheek when they haven't met for a long time, although hugging is common, even between men. When meeting someone for the first time, it's fine just to shake hands.

There are two forms of the word for "you", a formal or polite form, **vi** vee, which is also the plural and an informal form, **ti** tee, used for family, friends, children and animals. Notice that this changes in the expressions for "please" and "thank you". The informal greeting **bok** is used particularly in Zagreb.

The basics

bye	đenja *jenya*
excuse me	oprostite *(pl, sg polite) oprrosteetey;* oprosti *(sg inf) oprrostee*
good afternoon	dobar dan *dobarr dan*
goodbye	doviđenja *doveejenya*
good evening	dobar večer *dobarr vecherr*
good morning	dobro jutro *dobrro yootrro*
goodnight	laku noć *lakoo noch*
hello	zdravo *zdrravo*
hi	bok *bok*
no	ne *ney*
OK	OK *okey*
pardon	pardon *pardon,* ispričavam se *eesprreechavam se*
please	molim vas *(pl, sg polite) moleem vas;* molim te *(sg inf) moleem te*
thanks, thank you	hvala *Hvala*
yes	da *da*

Expressing yourself

I'd like …
želim …
zheleem …

we'd like …
želimo …
zheleemo …

do you want …?
hoćete li …?
Hochetey lee …?

do you have …?
imate li …?
eematey lee …?

is there a …?
ima li …?
eema li …?

are there any …?
ima li …?
eema li …?

how …?
kako …?
kako …?

why …?
zašto …?
zashto …?

when …?
kada …?
kada …?

what …?
što …?
shto …?

where is …?
gdje je …?
gdye yey …?

where are …?
gdje su …?
gdye soo …?

how much is it?
koliko to stoji?
koleeko to stoyee?

what is it?
što je to?
shto je to?

do you speak English?
govorite li engleski?
govorreetey lee engleskee?

where are the toilets, please?
molim vas, gdje je WC?
moleem vas, gdye yey vey tsey?

how are you?
kako ste?
kako stey?

fine, thanks
dobro, hvala
dobrro, Hvala

thanks very much
puno vam hvala
poono vam Hvala

no, thanks
ne, hvala
ney, Hvala

yes, please
da, molim
da, moleem

see you later
vidimo se kasnije
veedeemo sey kasneeyey

you're welcome
nema na čemu
nema na chemoo

I'm sorry
žao mi je
zhao mee yey

Understanding

besplatno	free
izlaz	exit
nemojte …	do not …
otvoreno	open
pozor	attention
rezervirano	reserved
u kvaru	out of order
ulaz	entrance
WC	toilets
zabranjeno parkiranje	no parking
zabranjeno pušenje	no smoking

tu je …/tu su …
there is …/there are …

dobro došli
welcome

da li vam smeta ako …?
do you mind if …?

trenutak, molim vas
one moment, please

molim vas sjednite
please take a seat

PROBLEMS UNDERSTANDING CROATIAN

Expressing yourself

pardon?
oprostite?
oprrosteetey?

what?
što?
shto?

could you repeat that, please?
možete li ponoviti, molim vas?
mozhetey lee ponoveetee, moleem vas?

could you speak more slowly?
možete li govoriti sporije, molim vas?
mozhetey lee govorreetee sporreeyey, moleem vas?

I don't understand
ne razumijem
ney rrazoomeeyem

I understand a little Croatian
malo razumijem hrvatski
malo rrazoomeeyem Hrrvatskee

I can understand Croatian but I can't speak it
razumijem hrvatski, ali ga ne znam govoriti
rrazoomeeyem Hrrvatskee, ali ga ne znam govorreetee

I hardly speak any Croatian
gotovo da i ne govorim hrvatski
gotovo da ee ne govoreem Hrrvatskee

do you speak English?
govorite li engleski?
govorreetey lee engleskee?

how do you say … in Croatian?
kako hrvatski kažete …?
kako Hrrvatskee kazhetey …?

how do you spell it?
kako to pišete?
kako to peeshetey?

what's that called in Croatian?
kako se ovo kaže hrvatski?
kako sey ovo kazhey Hrrvatskee?

could you write it down for me?
možete li mi to napisati, molim vas?
mozhetey lee mee to napeesatee, moleem vas?

Understanding

razumijete li hrvatski?
do you understand Croatian?

napisat ću vam to
I'll write it down for you

to znači …
it means …

to je neka vrsta …
it's a kind of …

SPEAKING ABOUT THE LANGUAGE

Expressing yourself

I learned a few words from my phrasebook
naučio *(m)*/naučila *(f)* sam nekoliko riječi iz udžbenika
naoocheeo/naoocheela sam nekoleeko reeyechee eez oodjbeneeka

I can just about get by
nekako se snalazim
nekako sey snalazeem

I hardly know two words!
samo natucam!
samo natootsam!

I find Croatian a difficult language
smatram da je hrvatski težak jezik
smatrram da yey Hrrvatskee tezhak yezeek

I know the basics but no more than that
znam osnove, ali ništa više od toga
znam osnovey, alee neeshta veeshey od toga

people speak too quickly for me
ljudi prebrzo govore
lyoodee prrebrrzo govorrey

Understanding

imate dobar naglasak
you have a good accent

jako dobro govorite
you speak very well

ASKING THE WAY

Expressing yourself

excuse me, can you tell me where the … is, please?
oprostite, možete li mi, molim vas, reći gdje je …?
oprrosteetey, mozhetey lee mee, moleem vas, rrechee gdyey yey …?

which way is it to …?
koji put vodi do …?
koyee poot vodee do …?

can you tell me how to get to …?
možete li mi reći kako doći do …?
mozhetey lee mee rrechee kako dochee do …?

is there a … near here?
ima li ovdje u blizini …?
eema lee ovdyey oo bleezeenee …?

could you show me on the map?
možete li mi to pokazati na karti?
mozhetey lee mee to pokazati na karrtee?

is there a map of the town somewhere?
može li se negdje naći plan grada?
mozhey lee sey negdyey nachee plan grrada?

is it far?
je li daleko?
yey lee daleko?

I'm looking for …
tražim …
trrazheem …

I'm lost
izgubio *(m)*/izgubila *(f)* sam se
eezgoobeeo/eezgoobeela sam se

Understanding

desno	right
idite dolje	go down
idite gore	go up
lijevo	left
nastavite tim putem	keep going
samo ravno	straight ahead
skrenite	turn
slijedite	follow

jeste li pješice?
are you on foot?

to je udaljeno pet minuta automobilom
it's five minutes away by car

to je prva/druga/treća ulica lijevo
it's the first/second/third on the left

na kružnom toku skrenite desno
turn right at the roundabout

skrenite lijevo kod banke
turn left at the bank

izađite na slijedećem izlazu
take the next exit

nije daleko
it's not far

tu je iza ugla
it's just round the corner

GETTING TO KNOW PEOPLE

The basics

bad	loše *loshey*
beautiful	lijepo *leeyepo*
boring	dosadno *dosadno*
cheap	jeftino *yefteeno*
expensive	skupo *skoopo*
good	dobro *dobrro*
great	divno *deevno*
interesting	zanimljivo *zaneemlyeevo*
nice	ugodno *oogodno*
not bad	nije loše *neeyey loshey*
well	dobro *dobrro*
to hate	mrziti *mrrzeetee*
to like	voljeti *volyetee*
to love	voljeti *volyetee*

INTRODUCING YOURSELF AND FINDING OUT ABOUT OTHER PEOPLE

Expressing yourself

my name's …
ime mi je …
eemey mee yey …

what's your name?
kako vam je ime?
kako vam yey eemey?

how do you do!
kako ste?
kako stey?

pleased to meet you!
drago mi je!
drrago mee yey!

this is my husband
ovo je moj suprug
ovo yey moy sooproog

this is my partner, Karen
ovo je moja partnerica Karen
ovo yey moya parrtnerreetsa Karen

I'm English
ja sam Englez *(m)*/Engleskinja *(f)*
ya sam englez/engleskeenya

we're Welsh
mi smo Welšani
mee smo velshanee

I'm from …
ja sam iz …
ya sam eez …

where are you from?
odakle ste?
odakley stey?

how old are you?
koliko vam je godina?
koleeko vam yey godeena?

I'm 22
meni su 22 godine
menee soo dvadeset dveeye godeeney

what do you do for a living?
kako zarađujete za život?
kako zarrajooyetey za zheevot?

are you a student?
studirate li?
stoodeerratey lee?

I work
radim
rradeem

I'm studying law
studiram pravo
stoodeerram prravo

I'm a teacher
učitelj *(m)*/učiteljica *(f)* sam
oocheetel'/oocheetelyeetsa sam

I stay at home with the children
ne radim, doma sam s djecom
ney rradeem, doma sam s dyetsom

I work part-time
radim skraćeno radno vrijeme
rradeem skrracheno rradno vrreeyemey

I work in marketing
radim u marketingu
rradeem oo marrketeengoo

I'm retired
u mirovini sam
oo meerroveenee sam

I'm self-employed
ja sam samozaposlenik *(m)*/samozaposlenica *(f)*
ya sam samozaposleneek/samozaposleneetsa

I have two children
imam dvoje djece
eemam dvoyey dyetsey

we don't have any children
nemamo djece
nemamo dyetsey

two boys and a girl
dva dječaka i djevojčicu
dva dyechaka ee dyevoycheetsoo

a boy of five and a girl of two
dječaku je pet, a djevojčici dvije godine
dyechakoo yey pet, a dyevoycheetsee dveeyey godiney

have you ever been to Britain?
jeste li ikada posjetili Veliku Britaniju?
yestey lee eekada posyeteelee veleekoo brreetaneeyoo?

jeste li Englez *(m)*/**Engleskinja** *(f)*?
are you English?

poznajem Englesku dosta dobro
I know England quite well

i mi smo ovdje na godišnjem odmoru
we're on holiday here too

volio *(m)*/**voljela** *(f)* **bih posjetiti Škotsku jednoga dana**
I'd love to go to Scotland one day

TALKING ABOUT YOUR STAY

Expressing yourself

I'm here on business
ovdje sam poslovno
ovdyey sam poslovno

we're on holiday
na godišnjem smo odmoru
na godeeshnyem smo odmorroo

I arrived three days ago
stigao *(m)*/stigla *(f)* sam prije tri dana
steegao/steegla sam prreeyey trree dana

we've been here for a week
ovdje smo već tjedan dana
ovdyey smo vech tyedan dana

I'm only here for a long weekend
ovdje sam na produženom vikendu
ovdyey sam na prrodoozhenom veekendoo

we're just passing through
u prolazu smo
oo prrolazoo smo

this is our first time in Croatia
po prvi put smo u Hrvatskoj
po prrvee poot smo oo Hrrvatskoy

we're here to celebrate our wedding anniversary
ovdje smo kako bismo proslavili godišnjicu braka
ovdye smo kako beesmo prroslaveelee godeeshnyeetsoo brraka

we're on our honeymoon
na medenom smo mjesecu
na medenom smo myesetsoo

we're here with friends
ovdje smo s prijateljima
ovdyey smo s prreeyatelyeema

we're touring around
kružimo okolo
krroozheemo okolo

we managed to get a cheap flight
uspjeli smo dobiti jeftin let
oospyelee smo dobeetee yefteen let

we're thinking about buying a house here
razmišljamo o kupovini kuće ovdje
rrazmeeshlyamo o koopoveenee koochey ovdyey

Understanding

uživajte u boravku!
enjoy your stay!

uživajte u ostatku odmora!
enjoy the rest of your holiday!

jeste li prvi put u Hrvatskoj?
is this your first time in Croatia?

koliko dugo ostajete?
how long are you staying?

sviđa li vam se ovdje?
do you like it here?

da li ste posjetili …?
have you been to …?

STAYING IN TOUCH

Expressing yourself

we should stay in touch
trebali bi ostati u vezi
trrebalee bee ostatee oo vezee

I'll give you my e-mail address
dat ću vam svoju e-mail adresu
dat choo vam svoyoo ee-mail adresoo

here's my address, if you ever come to Britain
evo moje adrese, ako ikada dođete u Britaniju
evo moyey adresey, ako eekada dojetey oo brreetaneeyoo

Understanding

hoćete li mi dati svoju adresu?
will you give me your address?

imate li e-mail adresu
do you have an e-mail address?

uvijek ste nam dobrodošli i možete kod nas odsjesti
you're always welcome to come and stay with us here

EXPRESSING YOUR OPINION

Expressing yourself

I really like ...
doista mi se sviđa ...
doeesta mee sey sveeja ...

I really liked ...
doista mi se svidjelo ...
doeesta mee sey sveedyelo ...

I don't like ...
ne sviđa mi se ...
ney sveeja mee sey ...

I didn't like ...
nije mi se svidjelo ...
neeyey mee se sveedyelo ...

I love ...
volim ...
voleem ...

I loved ...
volio *(m)*/voljela *(f)* sam ...
voleeo/volyela sam ...

I would like ...
želim ...
zheleem ...

I would have liked ...
želio *(m)*/željela *(f)* bih ...
zheleeo/zhelyela beeH ...

I find it ...
smatram da je to ...
smatrram da yey to ...

I found it ...
smatrao *(m)*/smatrala *(f)* sam da je ...
smatrrao/smatrrala sam da yey ...

18

it's lovely
zgodno je
zgodno yey

it was lovely
bilo je zgodno
beelo yey zgodno

I agree
slažem se
slazhem sey

I don't agree
ne slažem se
ney slazhem sey

I don't know
ne znam
ney znam

I don't mind
ne smeta me
ney smeta mey

I don't like the sound of it
ne sviđa mi se
ne sveeja mee sey

it sounds interesting
zvuči zanimljivo
zvoochee zaneemlyeevo

it really annoys me
to mi doista ide na živce
to mee doeesta eedey na zheevtsey

it was boring
bilo je dosadno
beelo yey dosadno

it's a rip-off
to je čista pljačka
to yey cheesta plyachka

it gets very busy at night
noću je pretrpano
nochoo yey prretrrpano

it's too busy
pretrpano je
prretrrpano yey

it's very quiet
jako je mirno
yako yey meerrno

I really enjoyed myself
doista sam se dobro proveo *(m)*/provela *(f)*
doeesta sam sey dobrro prroveo/prrovela

we had a great time
jako smo se dobro zabavili
yako smo sey dobrro zabaveelee

there was a really good atmosphere
ugođaj je doista bio odličan
oogojay yey doeesta beeo odlichan

we met some nice people
upoznali smo drage ljude
oopoznalee smo drragey lyoodey

we found a great hotel
otkrili smo odličan hotel
otkrreelee smo odleechan Hotel

Understanding

da li vam se sviđa?/volite li …?
do you like …?

jeste li se dobro zabavili?
did you enjoy yourselves?

trebali biste poći do …
you should go to …

mogu preporučiti …
I recommend …

to je jako zgodan predio
it's a lovely area

nema previše turista
there aren't too many tourists

nemojte ići za vikend, pretrpano je
don't go at the weekend, it's too busy

malo je precijenjeno
it's a bit overrated

TALKING ABOUT THE WEATHER

> **Some informal expressions**
>
> **lijevalo je k'o iz kabla** it was raining cats and dogs
> **pasja vrućina** it was a real scorcher
> **crkli smo od studeni** it was freezing

Expressing yourself

have you seen the weather forecast for tomorrow?
jeste li vidjeli vremensku prognozu za sutra?
yestey lee veedyelee vrremenskoo prrognozoo za sootra?

it's going to be nice
bit će lijepo
beet chey leeyepo

it isn't going to be nice
bit će ružno
beet chey rroozhno

it's really hot
doista je vruće
doeesta yey vrrooche

it gets cold at night
noću postaje hladnije
nochoo postayey Hladneeyey

the weather was beautiful
vrijeme je bilo lijepo
vrreeyemey yey beelo leeyepo

it rained a few times
kišilo je nekoliko puta
keesheelo je nekoleeko poota

there was a thunderstorm
bila je oluja
beela yey olooya

it's very humid here
ovdje je jako vlažno
ovdyey yey yako vlazhno

it's been lovely all week
vrijeme je bilo prekrasno cijeli tjedan
vrreeyemey yey beelo prrekrrasno tseeyelee tyedan

we've been lucky with the weather
vrijeme nas je poslužilo
vrreeyemey nas yey posloozheelo

Understanding

trebalo bi kišiti
it's supposed to rain

prognozirali su lijepo vrijeme do kraja tjedna
they've forecast good weather for the rest of the week

sutra će ponovno biti vruće
it'll be hot again tomorrow

TRAVELLING

The basics

airport	zračna luka *zrrachna looka*, aerodrom *aerrodrom*
boarding	ukrcavanje *ookrrtsavanye*
boarding card	karta za ukrcaj *karrta za ookrrtsay*
boat	brod *brrod*
bus	autobus *aootoboos*
bus station	autobusni kolodvor *aootoboosnee kolodvorr*
bus stop	autobusna postaja *aootoboosna postaya*
car	automobil *aootomobil*
check-in	registracija putnika *rregeestrratseeya pootnika*, check in *check in*
coach	autobus *aootoboos*
ferry	trajekt *trrayekt*
flight	let *let*
gate	izlaz na pistu *eezlaz na peestoo*
left-luggage (office)	garderoba *garrderoba*
luggage	prtljaga *prrtlyaga*
map	zemljopisna karta *zemlyopeesna karrta*
motorway	autocesta *aoototsesta*
passport	putovnica *pootovnitsa*
plane	zrakoplov *zrrakoplov*, avion *aveeon*
platform	peron *perron*
railway station	kolodvor *kolodvorr*
return (ticket)	povratna karta *povrratna karrta*
road	cesta *tsesta*
shuttle bus	autobus za posebne vožnje *aootobus za posebney vozhnyey*
single (ticket)	karta u jednom smjeru *karrta oo yednom smyerroo*
street	ulica *oolitsa*
streetmap	plan grada *plan grrada*
taxi	taxi *taksee*
terminal	terminal *terrmeenal*
ticket	karta *karrta*
timetable	red vožnje *rred vozhnyey*

town centre	centar grada *tsentarr grrada*
train	vlak *vlak*
tram	tramvaj *trramvay*
to book	rezervirati *rezerrveerratee*
to hire	unajmiti *oonaymeetee*, iznajmiti *eeznaymeetee*

Expressing yourself

where can I buy tickets?
gdje mogu kupiti karte?
gdye mogoo koopeetee karrte?

a ticket to ..., please
kartu do ... molim vas
karrtoo do ... moleem vas

I'd like to book a ticket
želim rezervirati kartu
zheleem rrezerrveerratee karrtoo

how much is a ticket to ...?
koliko stoji karta do ...?
koleeko stoyee karrta do ...?

are there any concessions for students?
imaju li studenti popust?
eemayoo lee stoodenti popoost?

could I have a timetable, please?
mogu li dobiti red vožnje, molim vas?
mogoo lee dobeetee rred vozhnyey, moleem vas?

is there an earlier/later train/plane/bus?
postoji li neki raniji/kasniji vlak/zrakoplov/autobus?
postoyee lee nekee rraneeyee vlak/zrrakoplov/aootoboos?

how long does the journey take?
koliko dugo traje putovanje?
koleeko doogo trrayey pootovanye?

is this seat free?
je li ovo mjesto slobodno?
yey lee ovo myesto slobodno?

I'm sorry, there's someone sitting there
žao mi je, netko već sjedi ovdje
zhao mee yey, netko vech syedee ovdyey

Understanding

Making sense of abbreviations
Nowadays many signs use pictorial symbols, but here are some abbreviations you may find on timetables, on arrivals and departures boards and when travelling around Croatia:

dol = dolazak arrival
FKK = Freikörperkultur nudist beach
HAC = hrvatske autoceste Croatian motorways
HAK = hrvatski akademski klub breakdown service
HŽ = hrvatske željeznice Croatian rail transport
HP = hrvatska pošta Croatian postal service
pol = polazak departure

Days of the week
po = ponedjeljak Monday
ut = utorak Tuesday
sr = srijeda Wednesday
čet = četvrtak Thursday
pet = petak Friday
sub = subota Saturday
ned = nedjelja Sunday

dolasci	arrivals
informacije	information
izlaz	exit
karte	tickets
muški WC	gents
odlasci	departures
ukinuta linija	cancelled
ulaz	entrance
u zakašnjenju	delayed
veza	connections
WC	toilets
zabranjen ulaz	no entry
ženski WC	ladies

TRAVELLING

sva su mjesta popunjena
everything is fully booked

BY PLANE

From April to October, Croatia Airlines operates two direct flights a week from Zagreb to Split and Dubrovnik. During the summer months, there is also a daily service between Zagreb and Brač island. In addition to Croatia Airlines, most major European airlines fly regularly between the UK and Croatia, including the budget airlines Easyjet (to Ljubljana) and Ryanair (to Trieste and Graz).

Expressing yourself

where's the British Airways check-in?
gdje je registriranje putnika/check in za British Airways?
gdye yey registrreeranye pootnika za british airways?

I've got an e-ticket
imam elektronsku kartu
eemam elektrronskoo karrtoo

one suitcase and one piece of hand luggage
jedan kofer i jedan komad ručne prtljage
yedan koferr ee yedan komad roochney prrtlyagey

what time do we board?
kada se ukrcavamo?
kada se ookrrtsavamo?

I'd like to confirm my return flight
želim potvrditi povratnu kartu
zheleem potvrrdeetee povrratnoo karrtoo

one of my suitcases is missing
nestao mi je kofer
nestao mee ye koferr

my luggage hasn't arrived
nije mi stigla prtljaga
neeye mee steegla prrtlyaga

the plane was two hours late
zrakoplov je kasnio dva sata
zrrakoplov yey kasneeo dva sata

I've missed my connection
propustio *(m)*/propustila *(f)* sam avion na koji sam trebao *(m)*/trebala *(f)*
  presjesti
*prropoosteeo/prropoosteela sam aveeon na koye sam trrebao/trrebala
  prresyestee*

I've left something on the plane
ostalo mi je nešto u zrakoplovu
ostalo mee yey neshto oo zrrakoplovoo

I want to report the loss of my luggage
želim prijaviti nestanak prtljage
zheleem prreeyaveetee nestanak prrtlyagey

Understanding

artikli koje treba prijaviti	goods to declare
bescarinska	duty free
carinska kontrola	customs
čekaonica za polaske	departure lounge
kontrola putovnica	passport control
neposredni ukrcaj	immediate boarding
ništa za prijaviti	nothing to declare
povrat prtljage	baggage reclaim
registracija putnika	check-in
tuzemni letovi	domestic flights

molimo, čekajte u čekaonici za polaske
please wait in the departure lounge

želite li sjedište uz prozor ili u srednjem redu?
would you like a window seat or an aisle seat?

morate presjesti u …
you'll have to change in …

koliko torbi imate?
how many bags do you have?

da li ste sve sami pakirali?
did you pack all your bags yourself?

da li vam je itko dao nešto za ponijeti u zrakoplov?
has anyone given you anything to take onboard?

prtljaga vam je pet kilograma teža od dozvoljenog
your luggage is five kilos overweight

izvolite kartu za ukrcaj　　　　**ukrcaj počinje u …**
here's your boarding card　　　　boarding will begin at …

molimo, krenite prema izlazu na pistu broj …
please proceed to gate number …

posljednji poziv za …
this is a final call for …

možete nazvati ovaj broj kako biste provjerili da li vam je stigla prtljaga
you can call this number to check if your luggage has arrived

BY TRAIN, COACH, BUS, TRAM

From Zagreb there are rail links to Osijek, Slavonski Brod, Vinkovci, Rijeka, Lupoglav and Pula (tickets can be bought from the station desks). An InterRail card lets you travel free on all second-class services across the whole Croatian rail network, with no age restrictions. The train and coach stations in Zagreb are very close together.

The cheapest way to get around Croatia is by coach. Information on times and connections is available at coach stations.

There is no underground system in Croatia. There are a few trams in Zagreb, but in most cities public transport is by bus. You can buy tickets from the driver or from newspaper kiosks.

For information about the coach network, see www.croatia.hr

Expressing yourself

what time is the next train to …?
kada polazi slijedeći vlak za …?
kada polazee sleeyedechee vlak za … ?

what time is the last train?
kada ide posljednji vlak?
kada eedey poslyednyee vlak?

which platform is it for …?
na kojem je peronu vlak za …?
na koyem yey perronoo vlak za …?

where can I catch a bus to …?
gdje mogu sjesti na autobus za …?
gdye mogoo syestee na aootoboos za …?

which line do I take to get to …?
kojom linijom trebam ići do …?
koyom leeneeeyom trrebam eechee do …?

is this the stop for …?
je li ovo postaja za …?
ye lee ovo postaya za …?

is this where the coach leaves for …?
je li ovo mjesto s kojeg polazi autobus za …?
ye lee ovo myesto s koyeg polazee aootoboos za …?

can you tell me when I need to get off?
možete li mi reći gdje moram izaći?
mozhetey lee mee rrechee gdye morram eezachee?

I've missed my train/bus
zakasnio *(m)*/zakasnila *(f)* sam na vlak/autobus
zakasneeo/zakasneela sam na vlak/aootoboos

Understanding

blagajna	ticket office
dnevno	for the day
dnevnu kartu, molim vas	tickets for travel today
mjesečno	monthly
prema vlakovima	to the trains
rezervacije	bookings
tjedno	weekly

postaja se nalazi malo dalje s desne strane
there's a stop a bit further along on the right

samo točan iznos, molim vas
exact money only, please

morate presjesti u …
you'll have to change at …

morate sjesti na autobus broj …
you need to get the number … bus

ovaj vlak stoji u …
this train calls at …

dvije postaje odavde
two stops from here

BY CAR

Your UK driving licence is valid for up to six months from your entry into Croatia. You must show your car insurance and registration documents at the border. The wearing of seatbelts is compulsory in both front and back. You must insure your car for Croatia, otherwise you will have to pay for insurance on the spot. Speed limits are 50 km/h in towns, 80 km/h out of town and 130 km/h on motorways. Motorways have exit tolls – for more information about motorway tolls, see www.croatia.hr. Four-star petrol is called **super**, unleaded is **bezolovni benzin** and diesel **dizel** or **nafta**.

Taxis are quite cheap and drivers are usually friendly and happy to answer your questions.

Hitch-hiking is reasonably safe on roads leading to the coast and the Riviera.

Expressing yourself

where can I find a service station?
gdje mogu naći benzinsku crpku?
gdye mogoo nachee benzeenskoo tsrrpkoo?

lead-free petrol, please
bezolovni benzin, molim vas
bezolovnee benzeen, moleem vas

how much is it per litre?
koliko stoji litra?
koleeko stoyee leetrra?

we got stuck in a traffic jam
zaglavili smo se u prometu
zaglaveelee smo sey oo prrometoo

is there a garage near here?
ima li negdje u blizini automehaničarska radionica?
eema lee negdye oo bleezeenee aootomeHanicharrska rradeeoneetsa?

can you help us to push the car?
možete li nam pomoći gurati automobil?
mozhetey lee nam pomochee goorratee aootomobeel?

the battery's dead
akumulator je crkao
akoomoolatorr yey tsrrkao

I've broken down
pokvario mi se automobil
pokvarreeo mee sey aootomobeel

we've run out of petrol
ponestalo nam je benzina
ponestalo nam yey benzeena

I've got a puncture and my spare tyre is flat
probušena mi je guma, a rezervna je prazna
prrobooshena mee yey gooma, a rezerrvna yey prrazna

we've just had an accident
upravo smo doživjeli prometnu nesreću
oopravo smo dozheevlyelee prrometnoo nesrrechoo

I've lost my car keys
izgubio *(m)*/izgubila *(f)* sam ključeve automobila
eezgoobeeo/eezgoobeela sam klyoochevey aootomobeela

how long will it take to repair?
koliko dugo će trajati popravak?
koleeko doogo chey trrayatee poprravak?

◆ Hiring a car

I'd like to hire a car for a week
želim unajmiti automobil na tjedan dana
zheleem oonaymeetee aootomobeel na tyedan dana

an automatic (car)
automobil s automatskim mjenjačem
aootomobeel s aootomatskeem myenyachem

I'd like to take out comprehensive insurance
želim kasko osiguranje
zheleem kasko oseegoorranye

◆ Getting a taxi

is there a taxi rank near here?
je li taxi postaja u blizini?
yey lee taksee postaya oo bleezeenee?

I'd like to go to ...
želim ići u ...
zheleem eechee oo ...

I'd like to book a taxi for 8pm
želim naručiti taxi za 20.00 sati
zheleem naroocheetee taksee za dvadeset satee

you can drop me off here, thanks
ovdje izlazim, hvala
ovdye eezlazeem, Hvala

how much will it be to go to the airport?
koliko bi stajala vožnja do zračne luke?
koleeko bee stayala vozhnya do zrrachne lookey?

◆ Hitchhiking

I'm going to ...
idem do ...
eedem do ...

can you drop me off here?
mogu li izaći ovdje?
mogoo lee eezachee ovdyey?

could you take me as far as ...?
možete li me odvesti do ...?
mozhetey lee mey odvestee do ...?

thanks for the lift
hvala na vožnji
Hvala na vozhnyee

we hitched a lift
stopirali smo
stopeeralee smo

Understanding

drugi pravci	other directions
ima slobodnih mjesta	spaces *(car park)*
lagano	slow
parkiralište	car park
plati i izloži	pay and display
popunjeno	full *(car park)*
sačuvajte kartu	keep your ticket
svi pravci	all directions
vozi trakom	get in lane
zabranjeno parkiranje	no parking

potrebna mi je vaša vozačka dozvola, neki drugi identifikacijski dokument, dokaz adrese i kreditna kartica
I'll need your driving licence, another form of ID, proof of address and your credit card

valja dati 1500 kuna pologa
there's a 1,500-kuna deposit

u redu, uđite odvest ću vas do …
alright, get in, I'll take you as far as …

BY BOAT

In summer, there is heavy traffic on the Croatian coast and the marinas are full of small private boats. There are two types of line: fast intercity lines and international lines, mainly linking Croatia and Italy. In summer, it is advisable to book your ticket in advance from one of the shipping companies.

The SMC company has daily crossings between Ancona in Italy and Šibenik, Zadar, Split and the islands of Vis and Korčula. Jadrolinija sails daily between Bari in Italy and Dubrovnik. There are also regular crossings between Venice and Pula. For more information about car ferries, see www.croatia.hr

Expressing yourself

how long is the crossing?
koliko dugo traje prijelaz?
koleeko doogo trrayey prreeyelaz?

I'm seasick
imam morsku bolest
eemam morrskoo bolest

Understanding

samo za nemotorizirane putnike	foot passengers only
slijedeći prijelaz je u …	next crossing at …

ACCOMMODATION

There are many different kinds of accommodation available, and prices are similar whether you are on the coast or inland. When travelling to very touristy areas like Dubrovnik and Korčula Island, it's best to book ahead with a travel agent.

When you arrive you will usually be asked for your passport, which will be returned to you when you leave. Prices displayed include taxes. You should be able to pay by credit card in hotels, but it's best to check first. However, on campsites and in private houses you will usually have to pay in cash.

Hotels are ranked by category: category A is equivalent to a 3- or 4-star hotel, while categories B and C are 2-star.

A cheaper option is to stay in a private home, which is common practice in Croatia. Look out for the multilingual signs saying **Sobe Zimmer Rooms**, which are everywhere in tourist areas, or ask at the tourist information office. Note that in high season, prices can go up by 20 to 30 percent. You can haggle over the price of the room, especially if you are staying for a week or more.

There are plenty of campsites which charge very reasonable rates. Nudist camps are common in Istria – they are usually found in more isolated areas.

There are only a few youth hostels in Croatia, situated in Dubrovnik, Korčula, Pula, Krk, Zadar and Zagreb.

The basics

bath	kada *kada*
bathroom	kupaonica *koopaoneetsa*
bathroom with shower	kupaonica s tušem *koopaoneetsa s tooshem*
bed	krevet *krrevet*
bed and breakfast	noćenje s doručkom *nochenye s dorroochkom*
cable television	kablovska televizija *kablovska televeezeeya*

campsite	kamp *kamp*
caravan	prikolica *prreekoleetsa*
cottage	kućica *koocheetsa*
double bed	bračni krevet *brrachnee krrevet*
double room	dvokrevetna soba *dvokrrevetna soba*
en-suite bathroom	soba s kupaonicom *soba s koopaoneetsom*
family room	obiteljska soba *obeetelyska soba*
flat	stan *stan*
full-board	pansion *panseeon*
fully inclusive	sve uključeno *svey ooklyoocheno*
half-board	polupansion *poloopanseeon*
hotel	hotel *Hotel*
key	ključ *klyooch*
self-catering	apartman *aparrtman*
shower	tuš *toosh*
single bed	krevet za jednu osobu *krrevet za yednoo osoboo*
single room	jednokrevetna soba *yednokrrevetna soba*
tenant	stanar *stanarr*
tent	šator *shatorr*
toilets	WC *vey tsey*
youth hostel	omladinski hotel *omladeenskee Hotel*
to book	rezervirati *rrezerrveerratate*
to rent	unajmiti *oonaymeetee*, iznajmiti *eeznaymeetee*
to reserve	rezervirati *rezerrveeratate*

ACCOMMODATION

Expressing yourself

I have a reservation
imam rezervaciju
eemam rrezerrvatseeyoo

the name's …
na ime …
na eemey …

do you take credit cards?
primate li kreditne kartice?
prreematey lee krredeetney karrteetsey?

Understanding

| nije sve popunjeno | vacancies |
| popunjeno je | full |

35

privatno private
recepcija reception
WC toilets

vašu putovnicu, molim vas
could I see your passport, please

molim vas ispunite ovaj formular
could you fill in this form?

HOTELS

Expressing yourself

do you have any vacancies?
imate li išta slobodno?
eematey lee eeshta slobodno?

how much is a double room per night?
koliko stoji noćenje u dvokrevetnoj sobi?
koleeko stoyee nochenyey oo dvokrrevetnoy sobee?

I'd like to reserve a double room/a single room for three nights
želim rezervirati dvokrevetnu/jednokrevetnu sobu za tri noćenja
zheleem rrezerrveerratee dvokrrevetnoo/yednokrrevetnoo soboo za trree nochenya

would it be possible to stay an extra night?
da li je moguće prespavati još jednu noć?
da lee yey mogoochey prrespavatee yosh yednoo noch?

do you have any rooms available for tonight?
imate li ijednu slobodnu sobu za noćas?
eematey lee eeyednoo slobodnoo soboo za nochas?

do you have any family rooms?
imate li obiteljskih soba?
eematey lee obeetelyskeeH soba?

would it be possible to add an extra bed?
da li je moguće dodati još jedan krevet?
da lee yey mogoochey dodatee yosh yedan krrevet?

could I see the room first?
mogu li prvo pogledati sobu?
mogoo lee prrvo pogledatee soboo?

do you have anything bigger/quieter?
imate li išta veće/mirnije?
eematey lee eeshta vechey/meerrneeyey?

that's fine, I'll take it
u redu je, ostat ću
oo redoo yey, ostat choo

could you recommend any other hotels?
možete li mi preporučiti neki drugi hotel?
mozhetey lee mee prreporroocheetee nekee drroogee Hotel?

is breakfast included?
da li je doručak uključen?
da lee yey dorroochak ooklyoochen?

what time do you serve breakfast?
u koje vrijeme poslužujete doručak?
oo koyey vrreeyemey posloozhooyetey dorroochak?

is there a lift?
ima li dizalo?
eema lee deezalo?

is the hotel near the centre of town?
da li je hotel u blizini centra grada?
da lee yey Hotel oo bleezeenee tsentrra grrada?

what time will the room be ready?
u koje će vrijeme soba biti spremna?
oo koyey chey vrreeyemey soba beetee sprremna?

the key for room …, please
ključ od sobe … molim vas
klyooch od sobey … moleem vas

could I have an extra blanket?
mogu li dobiti dodatni pokrivač?
mogoo lee dobeetee dodatnee pokrreevach?

the air conditioning isn't working
klima uređaj ne radi
kleema oorrejay ney rradee

Understanding

žao mi je, ali sve je popunjeno
I'm sorry, but we're full

imamo samo jednokrevetnu sobu
we only have a single room available

za koliko je to noći?
how many nights is it for?

vaše ime, molim vas
what's your name, please?

u sobu možete ući nakon podneva
check-in is from midday

sobu valja napustiti prije 11 sati
you have to check out before 11am

doručak poslužujemo u restoranu od 7.30 do 9.00 sati
breakfast is served in the restaurant between 7.30 and 9.00

da li biste željeli novine ujutro?
would you like a newspaper in the morning?

vaša soba još nije spremna
your room isn't ready yet

ovdje možete ostaviti prtljagu
you can leave your bags here

YOUTH HOSTELS

Expressing yourself

do you have space for two people for tonight?
možete li smjestiti dvoje ljudi za noćas?
mozhetey lee smyesteetee dvoyey lyoodee za nochas?

we've booked two beds for three nights
rezervirali smo dva kreveta za tri noći
rreserrveerralee smo dva krreveta za trree nochee

could I leave my backpack at reception?
mogu li na recepciji ostaviti svoj ruksak?
mogoo lee na retseptseeyee ostaveetee svoy rooksak?

do you have somewhere we could leave our bikes?
postoji li neko mjesto na kojem možemo ostaviti bicikle?
postoyee lee neko myesto na koyem mozhemo ostaveetee beetseekley?

I'll come back for it around 7pm
svratit ću po to oko 19 sati
svrrateet choo po to oko devetnayst satee

there's no hot water	**the sink's blocked**
nema tople vode	umivaonik je začepljen
nema topley vodey	*oomeevaoneek yey zacheplyen*

Understanding

imate li člansku iskaznicu?
do you have a membership card?

posteljina osigurana
bed linen is provided

hostel se ponovno otvara u 18.00 sati
the hostel reopens at 6 pm

SELF-CATERING

Expressing yourself

we're looking for somewhere to rent near a town
želimo unajmiti nešto u blizini grada
zheleemo oonaymeetee neshto oo bleezeenee grrada

where do we pick up/leave the keys?
gdje možemo podići/ostaviti ključeve?
gdyey mozhemo podeechee/ostaveetee klyoochevey?

is electricity included in the price?
da li je potrošak struje uključen u cijenu?
da lee yey potrroshak strrooyey ooklyoochen oo tseeyenoo?

are bed linen and towels provided?
dobivamo li posteljinu i ručnike?
dobeevamo lee postelyeenoo ee roochneekey?

is a car necessary?
da li je automobil neophodan?
da lee yey aootomobeel neopHodan?

is there a pool?
ima li bazen?
eema lee bazen?

is the accommodation suitable for elderly people?
da li smještaj odgovara potrebama starijih osoba?
da lee smyeshtay odgovarra potrrebama starreeyeeH osoba?

where is the nearest supermarket?
gdje je najbliže samoposluživanje?
gdyey yey naybleezhey samoposloozheevanyey?

Understanding

molimo vas ostavite kuću u prvobitnom stanju
please leave the house clean and tidy after you leave

kuća je kompletno namještena
the house is fully furnished

sve je uključeno u cijenu
everything is included in the price

u ovom vam kraju doista treba automobil
you really need a car in this part of the country

CAMPING

Expressing yourself

is there a campsite near here?
ima li negdje kamp u blizini?
eema lee negdyey kamp oo bleezeenee?

I'd like to book a space for a two-person tent for three nights
želim rezervirati mjesto za šator za dvije osobe za tri noćenja
zheleem rrezerrveerratee myesto za shatorr za dveeyey osobey za trree nochenya

how much is it a night?
koliko stoji noćenje?
koleeko stoyee nochenyey?

where is the shower block?
gdje se nalazi sanitarni čvor?
gdyey sey nalazee saneetarrnee chvor?

can we pay, please? we were at space …
možemo li platiti, molim vas? boravili smo na kamp mjestu …
mozhemo lee plateetee, moleem vas? Borraveelee smo na kamp myestoo …

Understanding

to stoji … za jedno noćenje po osobi
it's … per person per night

ako vam išta zatreba, samo nas pitajte
if you need anything, just come and ask

It's best to take cash when eating out – some restaurants do take credit cards, but it's not the norm. Be warned that wine can easily double your bill. You can order house wine (**gazdino vino**) if the restaurant offers it.

You can also buy food from street vendors, who sell all kinds of snacks like sausage sandwiches (**kobasice**), fried fish (**girice**) and ice creams (**sladoled**).

Croatians love to sit out at the pavement cafés which are popping up in every town. Prices are usually the same whether you sit outside or at the bar, and service is included.

It's the custom to drink coffee after meals and when taking a break during the day. Although all the cafés and restaurants now have espresso machines, the local preference is still for strong Turkish coffee.

Sok is the generic name for cordials and fruit juices. Thick fruit juices are called **gusti sok** (peach, strawberry or apricot juices) and orange juice is known as **djus**.

Wine (**vino**) is grown in several regions of Croatia: the Adriatic coast and the islands produce some full-bodied reds (**Dingač** from the Pelješac peninsula, **Teran** from Istria), and there are various whites (**Malvasia** from Istria, as well as **Pošip**, **Pinot** and **Muškat**). As it gets so hot in summer, wine is often diluted with water, creating drinks with new names: **bevanda** is red wine with still water, and **špricer** or **gemišt** is white wine spritzer (with sparkling water).

The most popular beers are **Karlovačko pivo** (from the Karlovac brewery) and **Ožujsko pivo** (from Zagreb), which are available both bottled and on tap.

The Croatian speciality is a spirit called **rakija**, which is drunk as an apéritif, with coffee or after a meal. There are various types: **šljivovica** is made from plums and **loza** from grapes, and **travarica** is herb-flavoured.

The basics

beer	pivo *peevo*
bill	račun *rachoon*
black coffee	crna kava *tsrrrna kava*
bottle	boca *botsa*
bread	kruh *krrooH*
breakfast	doručak *dorroochak*
coffee	kava *kava*
Coke®	Coca Cola *koka kola*
dessert	desert *desert*
dinner	večera *vecherra*
fruit juice	voćni sok *vochnee sok*
lemonade	limunada *leemoonada*
lunch	ručak *roochak*
main course	glavno jelo *glavno yelo*
menu	jelovnik *yelovneek*
mineral water	mineralna voda *meenerralna voda*
red wine	crno vino *tsrrno veeno*
rosé wine	ružica *roozhitsa*
salad	salata *salata*
sandwich	sendvič *sendveech*
service	posluživanje *posloozheevanyey*
sparkling *(water, wine)*	gaziran *gazeerran*
starter	predjelo *prredyelo*
still *(water)*	negazirana *negazeerrana*
tea	čaj *chay*
tip	napojnica *napoyneetsa*
water	voda *voda*
white coffee	bijela kava *beeyela kava*
white wine	bijelo vino *beeyelo veeno*
wine	vino *veeno*
wine list	vinska lista *veenska leesta*
to eat	jesti *yestee*
to have breakfast	doručkovati *dorroochkovatee*
to have dinner	večerati *vecherratee*
to have lunch	ručati *roochatee*

Expressing yourself

shall we go and have something to eat?
kako bi bilo da odemo nešto pojesti?
kako bee beelo da odemo neshto poyestee?

do you want to go for a drink?
želiš li poći na piće?
zheleesh lee pochee na peechey?

can you recommend a good restaurant?
možete li preporučiti dobar restoran?
mozhetey lee prreporroocheetee dobarr rrestorran?

I'm not very hungry
nisam jako gladan *(m)*/gladna *(f)*
neesam yako gladan/gladna

excuse me! *(to call the waiter)*
molim vas!
moleem vas!

cheers!
živjeli!
zheevyelee!

that was lovely
bilo je krasno
beelo yey krrasno

could you bring us an ashtray, please?
možete li nam donijeti pepeljaru, molim vas?
mozhetey lee nam doneeyetee pepelyaroo, moleem vas?

where are the toilets, please?
gdje je WC, molim vas?
gdyey yey vey tsey, moleem vas?

Understanding

za van/dostava u kuću takeaway

žao mi je, prestajemo posluživati u 23.00 sata
I'm sorry, we stop serving at 11pm

RESERVING A TABLE

Expressing yourself

I'd like to reserve a table for tomorrow evening
želim rezervirati stol za sutra uvečer
zheleem rrezerrveerratee stol za sootrra oovecher

for two people
za dvije osobe
za dveeyey osobey

around 8 o'clock
oko 20.00 sati
oko dvadeset satee

do you have a table available any earlier than that?
imate li slobodan stol ranije od toga?
eematey lee slobodan stol rraneeyey od toga?

I've reserved a table – the name's …
rezervirao *(m)*/rezervirala *(m)* sam stol – na ime …
rrezerrveerrao/rrezerrveerrala sam stol – na eemey …

Understanding

rezervirano
reserved

za koje vrijeme?
for what time?

na koje ime?
what's the name?

imate li rezervaciju?
do you have a reservation?

koliko osoba?
for how many people?

za pušače ili nepušače?
smoking or non-smoking?

da li vam ovaj stol u kutu odgovara?
is this table in the corner OK for you?

bojim se da je u ovom trenutku sve zauzeto
I'm afraid we're full at the moment

ORDERING FOOD

yes, we're ready to order
da, možemo naručiti
da, mozhemo narroocheetee

no, could you give us a few more minutes?
možete li nas pričekati još koji trenutak?
mozhetey lee nas prreechekatee josh koyee trrenootak?

I'd like ...
želim ...
zheleem ...

could I have ...?
mogu li dobiti ...?
mogoo lee dobeetee ...?

I'm not sure, what's "pašticada"?
još ne znam, što je "pašticada"?
yosh ney znam, shto yey pashteetsada?

I'll have that
to ću uzeti
to choo oozetee

does it come with vegetables?
da li u prilogu ima neko povrće?
da lee oo prreelogoo eema neko povrrchey?

what are today's specials?
što je ponuda dana?
shto yey ponooda dana?

what desserts do you have?
što imate za desert?
shto eematey za desert?

I'm allergic to nuts/wheat/seafood/citrus fruit
alergičan sam na orahe/žitarice/plodove mora/agrume
alerrgeechan (m)/alerrgeechna (f) sam na orraHey/jeetarreetzey/plodovey morra/agrroomey

some water, please
malo vode, molim vas
malo vodey, moleem vas

a bottle of red/white wine, please
bocu crnog/bijelog vina, molim vas
botsoo tsrrnog/beeyelog veena, moleem vas

that's for me
to je za mene
to yey za meney

this isn't what I ordered, I wanted …
to nije ono što sam naručio *(m)*/naručila *(f)*, htio/htjela sam …
to neeyey ono shto sam narroocheeo/narroocheela. Hteeo/Htyela sam …

could we have some more bread, please?
možemo li dobiti još kruha, molim vas?
mozhemo lee dobeetee josh krrooHa, moleem vas?

could you bring us another jug of water, please?
možete li nam donijeti još jedan vrč vode, molim vas?
mozhetey lee nam doneeyetee yosh yedan vrrch vodey, moleem vas?

Understanding

jeste li se odlučili što ćete naručiti?
are you ready to order?

vratit ću se za nekoliko trenutaka
I'll come back in a few minutes

žao mi je, nema više …
I'm sorry, we don't have any … left

što ćete popiti?
what would you like to drink?

želite li desert ili kavu?
would you like dessert or coffee?

je li sve bilo u redu?
was everything OK?

BARS AND CAFÉS

Expressing yourself

I'd like …
želim …
zheleem …

a Coke®/a diet Coke®
Coca Colu/dijetnu Coca Colu
koka koloo/deeyetnoo koka koloo

a glass of white/red wine
čašu bijelog/crnog vina
chashoo beeyelog/tsrrnog veena

a cup of tea
šalicu čaja
shalyeetsoo chaya

a cup of hot chocolate
šalicu vruće čokolade
shalyeetsoo vrroochey chokoladey

the same again, please
isto ponovno, molim vas
eesto ponovno, moleem vas

a black/white coffee
crnu/bijelu kavu
tsrrnoo/beeyeloo kavoo

a coffee and a croissant
kavu i pecivo
kavoo ee petseevo

Understanding

bezalkoholno
non-alcoholic

što želite
what would you like?

mogu li naplatiti, molim vas
could I ask you to pay now, please?

ovo je dio za nepušače
this is the non-smoking area

> **Some informal expressions**
> **biti mamuran/mamurna** to have a hangover
> **prejesti se** to have eaten too much

THE BILL

Expressing yourself

the bill, please
račun, molim vas
rrachoon, moleem vas

how much do I owe you?
koliko vam dugujem?
koleeko vam doogooyem?

do you take credit cards?
primate li kreditne kartice?
prreematey lee krredeetney karrteetsey?

I think there's a mistake in the bill
mislim da je došlo do pogreške u računu
meesleem da yey doshlo do pogrreshkey oo rachoonoo

is service included?
da li je posluživanje uključeno u cijenu?
da lee yey posloozheevanyey ooklyoocheno oo tseeyenoo?

Understanding

plaćate li zajedno?
are you all paying together?

da, posluživanje je uključeno
yes, service is included

Croatian cooking reflects the cultural mosaic of the country, a crossroads where the Latin, Slav, Byzantine and Austro-Hungarian worlds meet. Types of cooking vary according to region, with dishes from the North being richer and spicier than those in the South. Meals prepared for guests and special occasions in the villages tend to be abundant.

Normally, a meal consists of a starter (**predjelo**), a side dish (**prilog**), a main dish (**glavno jelo**) and a dessert (**desert**). **Pršut** (dried ham or prosciutto), served with goat's cheese and olives, is a common hors-d'oeuvre. This type of hors-d'oeuvre reminds one of Spanish tapas or Greek and Turkish mezze. Beer is popular among Croats, but the commonest accompaniment to a meal is wine.

Breakfast is generally savoury (cheese, ham, hard-boiled eggs) and often accompanied by coffee, black or white.

Lunch is the main meal of the day, served around 2–3pm. It usually consists of soup, meat, salad, bread or potatoes and a dessert, often a cake.

In urban areas, dinner is often cold (bread, cheeses and eggs), while in the country it is more likely to be a cooked meal.

In coastal regions, there is a pause in the middle of the morning for the famous **marenda**, a meal consisting of fish, cheese and bread. Small, light dishes may also be eaten in the middle of the day in other regions.

Understanding

dimljen	smoked
dobro pečeno	well done *(meat)*
hladan	cold
krvav	rare
kuhan	boiled, steamed
narezan	sliced
paniran	in breadcrumbs

pečen	roast
pečen na roštilju	grilled
pečen na žeravici	braised
pirjan	braised
popržen	sauté
pržen	fried
punjen	stuffed
rastopljen	melted
restan	sauté
srednje pečeno	well done *(meat)*
sušen	dried
svjež	fresh
začinjen	seasoned

◆ predjela starters

njoki od krumpira	gnocchi, potato dumplings
koktel od rakova i avokada	prawn and avocado cocktail
kulen	Slavonian sausage
omlet s gljivama	mushroom omelette
panirani sir	deep-fried cheese
paprika punjena sirom	peppers stuffed with cheese
paški sir u maslinovom ulju	Pag cheese marinated in olive oil
pašteta od pastrv	trout pâté
pašteta od tune	tuna pâté
piroške s ovčjim sirom	deep-fried fritter made from sheep's-milk cheese
rajčica punjena jajima	tomatoes stuffed with eggs
rotkvice i šampinjoni u jogurtu	radishes and mushrooms in yoghurt
štrukli od sira	cheese fritters
uštipci od mesa	meat fritters

◆ salate salads

krumpir salata	potato salad
kupus salata	cabbage salad
miješana salata	mixed salad
miješana salata s kupusom	mixed salad with cabbage
riblja salata	fish salad
salata od dinje	melon salad

salata od govedine	beef salad
salata od hobotnice	octopus salad
salata od lignji	squid salad
salata od luka	onion salad
salata od sipa	cuttlefish salad
salata od tune	tuna salad
zelena salata	green salad

◆ juhe soups

bečka gulaš-juha (govedina)	Viennese goulash soup (made with beef)
dalmatinska gulaš juha	thick Dalmatian soup
govedska juha	beef soup
gulaš juha s krumpirima	thick potato soup
janjeća juha	lamb soup
juha od povrća	vegetable soup
juha od rakova	prawn soup
juha od somove glave	catfish head soup
pileća juha	chicken soup
zagorska juha od krumpira	Zagorje potato soup

◆ ribe i morski proizvodi fish and sea food

bakalar s krumpirima	cod with potatoes
baranjski riblji paprikaš	Baranja fish stew
blitva s plodovima mora	chard with sea food
brodet od skuša	mackerel "brodetto" (thick soup)
buzara	scampi à la "buzara" (with breadcrumbs, garlic, parsley, wine and olive oil)
file od oslića	hake fillet
hobotnica ispod peke s mladim krumpirima	octopus with new potatoes
hobotnica na hvarski	octopus in the Hvar island style
jegulja na dalmatinski način	Dalmatian eel
lignje s krumpirom	squid with potatoes
marinada od jegulje	marinaded eels
marinada od ribe	marinaded fish

neretvanski brodet od jegulja i žaba	"brodetto" of eels and frogs from the Neretva river
oslić u listu tikvice	hake with courgettes
pastrva u vinu	trout in wine
pastrva sa šunkom	trout with ham
pečena hobotnica s krumpirom	grilled octopus with potatoes
pijani šaran	carp cooked in wine
pržena riba sa sirom	fried fish with cheese
pržene lignje	fried squid
pržene srdele	fried sardines
prženi somići	small fried catfish
punjena pastrva s roštilja	grilled stuffed trout
punjene lignje	stuffed squid
punjeni šaran	stuffed carp
riba u pivu	fish in beer sauce
riba u vinu	fish in wine sauce
riblji paprikaš	fish stew
rižoto crni	black risotto (with squid ink)
rižoto od škampa	scampi risotto
smuđ u češnjaku	perch with garlic
som sa šampinjonima	catfish with mushrooms
som u vinu	catfish with wine
stonske kamenice	Ston oysters
šaran u kajmaku	carp with cream sauce
škampi na roštilju	grilled scampi
skuše na lešo	steamed mackerel

◆ **jela s mesom** meat dishes

divljač s knedlima	game with dumplings
fazan u umaku od borovnice	pheasant in blueberry sauce
filani janjeći but	stuffed leg of lamb
gulaš s gljivama	mushroom goulash
istarski kaneloni	Istrian cannelloni (stuffed with meat)
janjetina na ražnju	spit-roast lamb
jaretina iz pećnice	roast kid
jelen u crnom pivu	venison in dark-beer sauce
koljenica na žaru	grilled leg of pork
kunić s gljivama	rabbit with mushrooms

FOOD AND DRINK

kutjevački srneći medaljoni	venison medallions (from Kutjevo)
narodni gulaš	traditional goulash
paška janjetina ispod peke	lamb baked in a pot, covered in hot coals
patka na mediteranski način	Mediterranean duck
pečena šunka	roast ham
kopun s orasima	chicken with walnuts
pileća jetrica	chicken liver
pileći minjoni u umaku	chicken pieces in sauce
pirjana teleća koljenica	braised leg of veal
punjena pileća prsa	stuffed chicken breast
punjeni odojak	stuffed suckling pig
pureći odrezak sa suhim šljivama	turkey cutlets with prunes
svinjsko pečenje u vinu	pork roasted in wine
šparoge sa šunkom	asparagus with ham
šunka pečena u tijestu	ham en croûte
teleća koljenica s grožđicama	leg of veal with raisins
teleća prsa u crnom vinu	veal breast with red wine
teleće pečenje	roast veal
teleći medaljoni i umak od gljiva	medallions of veal with mushroom sauce
teleći medaljoni u umaku	medallions of veal in sauce
teletina ispod peke	veal baked in a pot, covered in hot coals
vinski gulaš	goulash with wine

◆ desert desserts

božićni kolač s lješnjakom	Christmas cake with hazelnuts
čokoladne kuglice	chocolate balls
džem od lubenice	watermelon jam
jabuke s kremom	apples with cream
knedle sa šljivama	plum dumplings
kolač s makom	poppy-seed cake
kolač s orasima	walnut cake
palačinke	pancakes
pogača od jabuka	apple cake
rolada od kestena	chestnut roulade

rolada	roulade
smokve s medom i vinom	figs with honey and wine
sušene jabuke	dried apples
sušene šljive	prunes
štrudl s orasima	walnut strudel
štrukli s bademima	almond doughnuts
voćna salata u dinji	fruit salad served in half a melon

◆ **vina** wines

> The Croatian climate is ideal for the cultivation of vines. Wine is cheaper if you ask for the house wine (**gazdino vino**), which is generally very good. Croatian wines are often full-bodied, which is why, particularly in summer, locals often dilute them with still water (**bevanda**) or sparkling water (**gemišt**).

GLOSSARY OF FOOD AND DRINK

avokado avocado
bademi almonds
bajami almonds
bakalar cod
bevanda wine diluted with still water
blitva chard
borovnice blueberries
brodet "brodetto" (thick fish soup)
but thigh
celer celery
češnjak garlic
čokolada chocolate
dagnje mussels
dinja melon
divljač game
džem jam
fazan pheasant

fritule doughnuts, fritters
gemišt white wine diluted with sparkling water
gljive mushrooms
govedina beef
grožđe grapes
gulaš goulash
hobotnica octopus
jabuka apple
jaje egg
janjetina lamb
jaretina kid
jegulja eel
juha soup
kajmak kind of fresh cream cheese
kamenice oysters
kestenje chestnuts
kolač cake
koljenica shank

krumpir potato
kulen sausage
kunić rabbit
kupus cabbage
lignje squid
lješnjak hazelnut
loza grappa *(type of brandy)*
lubenica watermelon
luk onion
mak poppy seed
masline olives
med honey
mesne okruglice meatballs
meso meat
ocat vinegar
odojak suckling pig
odrezak escalope, steak
orasi walnuts
oslić hake
palačinke pancakes
papar pepper
paprika paprika
paprikaš paprika stew
paradajz tomato
pastrva trout
pašteta pâté
patka duck
peka pot (covered in hot coals)
peršun parsley
pijetao cock
piletina chicken
piroške doughnuts, fritters
pivo beer
povrće vegetables
rak crab

rakija brandy
ražnjići kebabs
riba fish
riža rice
rolada sweet roulade
roštilj grill
rotkvica radish
salata salad
sipa cuttlefish
sir cheese
sirup syrup
skuša mackerel
smokve figs
smuđ perch
sol salt
som catfish
srdele sardines
srna deer
srnetina venison
sušene šljive prunes
šaran carp
šećer sugar
škampi scampi
šljiva plum brandy
šparoge asparagus
štrudl strudel
šunka ham
tikvica courgette
tuna tuna
ulje oil
umak sauce
uštipci doughnuts, fritters
vino wine
voće fruit
žaba frog

Cultural information can be found at the tourist information office of your nearest city.

At the cinema, films are always shown in the original language with Croatian subtitles.

Theatre is very popular in Croatia, although many theatres are not open during the summer months. Do not miss the opportunity of seeing opera performed in the open in Diocletian's Palace in Split if you are there at the right time. The Dubrovnik Summer Festival offers a wealth of music and theatrical productions and it is worth seeing "Hamlet" performed on the Lovrijenac fortress by the city walls even if you do not know Croatian well.

The basics

ballet	balet *balet*
band	glazbeni sastav *glazbenee sastav*
bar	bar *barr*
cinema	kino *keeno*
circus	cirkus *tseerrkoos*
classical music	klasična glazba *klaseechna glazba*
club	disco *deesko*, klub *kloob*
concert	koncert *kontserrt*
dubbed film	sinkronizirani film *seenkroneezeeranee feelm*
festival	festival *festeeval*
film	film *feelm*
folk music	narodna glazba *narrodna glazba*
group	sastav *sastav*
jazz	džez *jez*
modern dance	suvremeni ples *soovrremenee ples*
musical	mjuzikl *myoozeekl*
party	zabava *zabava*
play	kazališna predstava *kazaleeshna prredstava*

pop music	pop glazba *pop glazba*
rock music	rock glazba *rok glazba*
show	predstava *prredstava*
subtitled film	titlovani film *teetlovanee feelm*
theatre	kazalište *kazaleeshtey*
ticket	ulaznica *oolazneetsa*
to book	rezervirati *rrezerrveerratee*
to go out	izlaziti *eezlazeetee*

SUGGESTIONS AND INVITATIONS

Expressing yourself

where can we go?
kamo možemo poći?
kamo mozhemo pochee?

what do you want to do?
što želiš *(m)*/želite *(f)* raditi?
shto zheleesh/zheleetey rradeetee?

shall we go for a drink?
hoćemo li na piće?
Hochemo lee na peechey?

what are you doing tonight?
što radiš večeras?
shto radeesh vecherras?

do you have plans?
imaš li kakvih planova?
eemash lee kakveeH planova?

would you like to …?
želiš li …?
zheleesh lee …?

we were thinking of going to …
htjeli smo otići do …
Htyelee smo oteechee do …

I can't today, but maybe some other time
ne mogu danas, možda neki drugi put
ney mogoo danas, mozhda nekee drroogee put

I'm not sure I can make it
nisam siguran *(m)*/sigurna *(f)* da ću moći
neesam seegoorran/seegoorrna da choo mochee

I'd love to
rado bih
rado beeH

ARRANGING TO MEET

Expressing yourself

what time shall we meet?
u koliko ćemo se sati naći?
oo koleeko chemo se satee nachee?

where shall we meet?
gdje ćemo se naći?
gdyey chemo sey nachee?

would it be possible to meet a bit later?
možemo li se naći malo kasnije?
mozhemo lee sey nachee malo kasneeyey?

I have to meet … at nine
moram se sastati s … u devet
morram sey sastatee s … oo devet

I don't know where it is but I'll find it on the map
ne znam gdje je to, ali naći ću na planu
ney znam gdyey yey to, alee nachee choo na planoo

see you tomorrow night
vidimo se sutra navečer
veedeemo sey sootrra navecherr

I'll meet you later, I have to stop by the hotel first
sastat ću se s tobom kasnije, moram prvo skočiti do hotela
sastat choo sey s tobom kasneeyey, morram prrvo skocheetee do Hotela

I'll call/text you if there's a change of plan
mogu te nazvati/poslati poruku ako dođe do promjene plana
mogoo tey nazvatee/poslatee porrookoo ako dojey do promyeney plana

are you going to eat beforehand?
hoćete li jesti prije toga?
Hochetey lee yestee prreeyey toga?

sorry I'm late
ispričavam se što kasnim
eesprreechavam sey shto kasneem

Understanding

da li se slažeš s time?
is that OK with you?

naći ćemo se tamo
I'll meet you there

doći ću po tebe oko 20.00 sati
I'll come and pick you up about 8

možemo se naći vani
we can meet outside

dat ću ti svoj broj pa me možeš sutra nazvati
I'll give you my number and you can call me tomorrow

> **Some informal expressions**
> **idemo nešto gucnuti?** shall we go out for a drink?
> **hoćemo li nešto prigristi?** shall we have a bite to eat?

FILMS, SHOWS AND CONCERTS

Expressing yourself

is there a guide to what's on?
imate li reperrtoar?
eematey lee rreperrtoarr?

two tickets, please
dvije ulaznice, molim vas
dveeyey oolazneetsey, moleem vas

I've seen the trailer
vidio *(m)*/vidjela *(f)* sam foršpan
veedeeo/veedyela sam forshpan

I'd like three tickets for …
molim vas tri ulaznice za …
moleem vas trree oolazneetsey za …

it's called …
naziv je …
nazeev yey …

what time does it start?
kada počinje?
kada pocheenyey?

I'd like to go and see a show
rado bih pogledao *(m)*/pogledala *(f)* predstavu
rrado beeH pogledao/pogledala prredstavoo

I'll find out whether there are still tickets available
pokušat ću doznati ima li još uvijek ulaznica
pokooshat choo doznatee eema lee yosh ooveeyek oolazneetsa

do we need to book in advance?
da li trebamo rezervirati karte?
da lee trrebamo rrezerrveerratee karrtey?

how long is it on for?
koliko će se dugo prikazivati?
koleeko chey sey doogo prreekazeevatee?

are there tickets for another day?
ima li ulaznica za neki drugi dan?
eema lee oolazneetsa za nekee drroogee dan?

I'd like to go to a bar with some live music
htio *(m)*/htjela *(f)* bih ići u bar s glazbom uživo
Hteeo/Htyela beeH eechee oo barr s glazbom uzheevo

are there any free concerts?
ima li ikakvih besplatnih koncerata?
eema lee eekakveeH besplatneeH kontserrata?

what sort of music is it?
kakva je ovo vrsta glazbe?
kakva yey ovo vrrsta glazbey?

Understanding

blagajna	box office
filmska uspješnica	blockbuster
kinematograf u kojem se prikazuju umjetnički filmovi	arthouse cinema
matineja	matinée
ograničena vidljivost	restricted view
prikazuje se od …	on general release from …
rezervacije	bookings

to je koncert na otvorenom
it's an open-air concert

kritike su bile jako dobre
it's had very good reviews

prikazuje se od slijedećeg tjedna
it comes out next week

prikazuje se od 20 sati u Tesla
it's on at 8pm at the Tesla

ova je predstava rasprodana
that showing's sold out

sve je rezervirano do …
it's all booked up until …

nije potrebno unaprijed rezervirati
there's no need to book in advance

predstava traje sat i pol zajedno s pauzom
the play lasts an hour and a half, including the interval

molimo isključite mobitele
please turn off your mobile phones

PARTIES AND CLUBS

Expressing yourself

I'm having a little leaving party tonight
pripremam malu oproštajnu zabavu večeras
prreeprremam maloo oprroshtaynoo zabavoo vecherras

should I bring something to drink?
trebam li donijeti neko piće?
trrebam lee doneeyetee neko peechey?

we could go to a club afterwards
možemo poslije toga otići u disco
mozhemo posleeyey toga oteechee oo deesko

do you have to pay to get in?
da li se ulaz plaća?
da lee sey oolaz placha?

I have to meet someone inside
moram se unutra naći s nekim
morram sey oonootrra nachee s nekeem

will you let me back in when I come back?
da li ćete me ponovno pustiti unutra ako izađem?
da lee chetey mey ponovno poosteetee oonootrra ako eezajem?

the DJ's really cool
dj je fantastičan
dee jey yey fantasteechan

do you come here often?
dolaziš li često ovdje?
dolazeesh lee chesto ovdyey?

can I buy you a drink?
mogu li te ponuditi pićem?
mogoo lee tey ponoodeetee peechem?

thanks, but I'm with my boyfriend
hvala, ali ovdje sam s dečkom
Hvala, alee ovdyey sam s dechkom

no thanks, I don't smoke
ne hvala, ne pušim
ne Hvala, ney poosheem

Understanding

besplatno piće
WC
7 kuna nakon ponoći

free drink
cloakroom
7 kuna after midnight

u Aninom stanu je zabava
there's a party at Anne's place

hoćeš li zaplesati?
do you want to dance?

mogu li te ponuditi pićem?
can I buy you a drink?

imaš li vatre?
have you got a light?

imaš li cigaretu?
have you got a cigarette?

možemo li se ponovno vidjeti?
can we see each other again?

mogu li te otpratiti kući?
can I see you home?

TOURISM AND SIGHTSEEING

ⓘ

The official Croatian tourism website, www.croatia.hr, offers a historical overview of each town and village, as well as the addresses of tourist information offices, lists of hotels, maps, opening hours, details of cultural events etc. All information is available in English.

There are no fewer than 48 marinas on the coast of Croatia. For information on sailing, see the Tourism PLUS – Nautics section of the website.

The basics

ancient	star *starr*
antique	drevan *drrevan*
area	područje *podrroochyey*
castle	dvorac *dvorrats*
cathedral	katedrala *katedrrala*
century	stoljeće *stolyechey*
church	crkva *tsrrkva*
exhibition	izložba *eezlozhba*
gallery	galerija *galerreeya*
modern art	suvremena umjetnost *soovrremena oomyetnost*
mosque	džamija *jameeya*
museum	muzej *moozey*
painting	slika *sleeka*
park	park *parrk*
ruins	ruševine *rroosheveeney*
sculpture	skulptura *skoolptoorra*
statue	statua *statooa*
street map	plan grada *plan grrada*
synagogue	sinagoga *seenagoga*
tour guide	vodič *vodeech*

tourist	turist *toorreest*
tourist information centre	turistički informacijski centar
	toorreesteechkee eenforrmatseeyskee tsentarr
town centre	centar grada *tsentarr grrada*

Expressing yourself

I'd like some information on …
želim neke pojedinosti o …
zheleem poyedeenostee o …

can you tell me where the tourist information centre is?
možete li mi reći gdje je turistički informacijski centar?
mozhetey lee mee rechee gdyey yey toorreesteechkee eenforrmatseeyskee tsentarr?

do you have a street map of the town?
imate li plan grada?
eematey lee plan grrada?

I was told there's an old abbey you can visit
rečeno mi je da postoji stara opatija koju se može posjetiti
rrecheno mee yey da postoyee starra opateeya koyoo sey mozhey posyeteetee

can you show me where it is on the map?
možete li mi, molim vas, na planu pokazati gdje se to nalazi?
mozhetey lee mee, moleem vas, na planoo pokazatee gdyey sey to nalazee?

how do you get there?
kako se dođe do tamo?
kako sey dojey do tamo?

is it free?
je li ulaz besplatan?
yey lee oolaz besplatan?

when was it built?
kada je izgrađen?
kada yey eezgrrajen?

Understanding

besplatan ulaz	admission free
gotičko	Gothic
invazija	invasion
nalazite se ovdje	you are here (on a map)
obilazak s vodičem	guided tour
obnavljanje	renovation
otvoreno	open
rat	war
restauracijski radovi	restoration work
rimsko	Roman
srednjovjekovno	medieval
stari grad	old town
zatvoreno	closed

morate pitati kada tamo dođete
you'll have to ask when you get there

slijedeći obilazak s vodičem počinje u 14.00 sati
the next guided tour starts at 2 o'clock

MUSEUMS, EXHIBITIONS AND MONUMENTS

Expressing yourself

I've heard there's a very good … exhibition on at the moment
čujem da ima jako dobra izložba … u ovom trenutku
chooyem da eema yako dobrra eezlozhba … oo ovom trrenootkoo

how much is it to get in?
koliko stoji ulaz?
koleeko stoyee oolaz?

is this ticket valid for the exhibition as well?
da li ova ulaznica vrijedi i za izložbu?
da lee ova oolazneetsa vrreeyedee ee za eezlozhboo?

are there any discounts for young people?
imaju li mladi kakav popust?
eemayoo lee mladee kakav popoost?

is it open on Sundays?
e li otvoreno nedjeljom?
vey lee otvorreno nedyelyom?

two concessions and one full price, please
dvije s popustom, a jednu po punoj cijeni, molim vas
dveeye s popoostom, a yednoo po poonoy tseeyenee, moleem vas

I have a student card
imam studentsku iskaznicu
eemam stoodentskoo eeskazneetsoo

Understanding

audiovodič	audioguide
blagajna	ticket office
molimo, ne dirajte	please do not touch
nije dozvoljena uporaba bljeskalice	no flash photography
nije dozvoljeno fotografiranje	no photography
ovuda	this way
privremena izložba	temporary exhibition
stalna izložba	permanent exhibition
tišina, molim	silence, please

ulaz u muzej stoji …
admission to the museum costs …

s istom ulaznicom možete razgledati i izložbu
this ticket also allows you access to the exhibition

imate li studentsku iskaznicu?
do you have your student card?

GIVING YOUR IMPRESSIONS

Expressing yourself

it's beautiful
lijepo je
leeyepo yey

it was beautiful
bilo je lijepo
beelo yey leeyepo

67

it's fantastic
fantastično je
fantasteechno yey

it was fantastic
bilo je fantastično
beelo yey fantasteechno

I really enjoyed it
doista sam uživao (m)/uživala (f)
doeesta sam oozheevao/oozheevala

I didn't like it that much
nije mi se baš svidjelo
neeyey mee se bash sveedyelo

it was a bit boring
bilo je pomalo dosadno
beelo yey pomalo dosadno

I'm not really a fan of modern art
ne ludujem za suvremenom umjetnošću
ney loodooyem za soovrremenom oomyetnoshchoo

it's expensive for what it is
preskupo je za ono što jest
prreskoopo yey za ono shto yest

it's very touristy
malo je previše turističko
malo yey prreveeshey tooreesteechko

it was really crowded
bilo je doista pretrpano
beelo yey doeesta prretrrpano

we didn't go in the end, the queue was too long
nismo na kraju otišli, red je bio predugačak
neesmo na krrayoo oteeshlee, red yey beeo prredoogachak

we didn't have time to see everything
nismo imali vremena sve razgledati
neesmo eemalee vrremena svey rrazgledatee

Understanding

čuveno	famous
slikovito	picturesque
tipično	typical
tradicionalno	traditional

morate svakako otići i pogledati ...
you really must go and see ...

preporučujem odlazak do ...
I recommend going to ...

odatle je fantastičan pogled na cijeli grad
there's a wonderful view over the whole city

postalo je malo previše turističko
it's become a bit too touristy

obala je posve uništena
the coast has been completely ruined

SPORTS AND GAMES

Football is one of the most popular sports in Croatia. The two rival teams are Dinamo Zagreb and Hajduk from Split. Their fans are nicknamed "The Bad Blue Boys" and "The Torcidas" respectively.

Other popular team sports include volleyball, basketball and water-polo.

There is an increasing number of cycle paths, particularly in Istria. Information is available from tourist information offices. In the Gorski Kotar region, near Rijeka, fans of the great outdoors can enjoy hiking, canoeing, white-water rafting and paragliding. You can find out all you need to know, including maps and a list of mountain refuges, at the Delnice tourist information office: see www.tz-delnice.hr (site available in English) or www.gorskikotar. com (Croatian only). Climbing and mountain biking are possible in the Paklenica national park, near Zadar (see www.paklenica.hr).

The basics

ball	lopta *lopta*
basketball	košarka *kosharrka*
board game	društvena igra *drrooshtvena eegrra*
cards	karte *karrtey*
chess	šah *shaH*
cross-country skiing	cross country skijanje *cross country skeeyanyey*
cycling	biciklizam *beetseekleezam*
downhill skiing	spust *spoost*
football	nogomet *nogomet*
hiking path	pješačka staza *pyeshachka staza*
match	utakmica *ootakmeetsa*
mountain biking	brdski biciklizam *brrdskee beetseekleezam*
play	igrati *eegrratee*
pool *(game)*	biljar *beelyarr*
rugby	ragbi *ragbee*

snowboarding	snowboarding *snowboarding*
sport	šport *shporrt*
surfing	surfanje *soorrfanyey*
swimming	plivanje *pleevanyey*
swimming pool	bazen za plivanje *bazen za pleevanyey*
table football	stolni nogomet *stolnee nogomet*
tennis	tenis *tenees*
trip	izlet *eezlet*
to go hiking	ići na rekreativno pješačenje *eechee na rrekrreateevno pyeshachenyey*
to have a game of ...	odigrati partiju ... *odeegrratee parrteeyoo ...*
to ski	skijati se *skeeyatee sey*

Expressing yourself

I'd like to hire ... for an hour
želim unajmiti ... na jedan sat
zheleem oonaymeetee ... na yedan sat

are there ... lessons available?
mogu li se uzeti satovi ...?
mogoo lee sey oozetee satovee ...?

how much is it per person per hour?
koliko to stoji na sat po osobi?
koleeko to stoyee na sat po osobee?

I'm not very sporty
nisam baš sportski tip
neesam bash sporrtskee teep

I've never done it before
nisam to prije činio *(m)*/činila *(f)*
neesam to prreeyey cheeneeo/cheeneela

I've done it once or twice, a long time ago
učinio *(m)*/učinila *(f)* sam to jedanput ili dvaput, ali to je bilo davno
oocheeneeo/oocheeneela sam to yedanpoot eelee dvapoot, alee to yey beelo davno

I'm exhausted!
iscrpljen (m)/iscrpljena (f) sam
eestsrrplyen/eestsrrplyena sam

I'd like to go and watch a football match
želim otići na nogometnu utakmicu
zheleem oteechee na nogometnoo ootakmeetsoo

shall we stop for a picnic?
da stanemo ovdje i piknikujemo?
da stanemo ovdyey ee peekneekooyemo?

we played ...
igrali smo ...
eegrralee smo ...

Understanding

.....za unajmiti   ... for hire

imate li iskustva ili ste/si početnik/početnica?
do you have any experience, or are you a complete beginner?

polog iznosi ...
there is a deposit of ...

osiguranje je obvezatno, a iznosi ...
insurance is compulsory and costs ...

HIKING

Expressing yourself

are there any hiking paths around here?
postoje li pješačke staze u blizini?
postoyey lee pyeshachkey stazey oo bleezeenee?

can you recommend any good walks in the area?
možete li preporučiti neku dobru pješačku stazu u okolici?
mozhetey lee prreporroocheetee nekoo dobrroo pyeshachkoo stazoo oo okoleetsee?

I've heard there's a nice walk by the lake
čuo sam kako uz jezero ima dobra pješačka staza
chuo sam kako ooz yezerro eema dobrra pyeshachka staza

we're looking for a short walk somewhere round here
tražimo mjesto za kratko pješačenje u blizini
trrazheemo myesto za krratko pyeshachenyey oo bleezeenee

can I hire hiking boots?
mogu li unajmiti gojzerice?
mogoo lee oonaymeetee goyzerreetsey?

how long does the hike take?
koliko dugo traje pješačenje?
koleeko doogo trrayey pyeshachenyey?

is it very steep?
je li jako strmo?
yey lee yako strrmo?

where's the start of the path?
gdje je početak staze?
gdyey yey pochetak stazey?

is the path waymarked?
je li staza označena?
yey lee staza oznachena?

is it a circular path?
je li staza kružna?
yey lee staza krroozhna?

Understanding

prosječno trajanje   average duration *(of walk)*

to je tri sata hodanja uključivši i stanke za odmor
it's about three hours' walk including rest stops

ponesite nepromočivu vjetrovku i gojzerice
bring a waterproof jacket and some walking shoes

SKIING AND SNOWBOARDING

Expressing yourself

I'd like to hire skis, poles and boots
želim unajmiti skije, štapove i pancerice
zheleem oonaymeetee skeeyey, shtapovey ee pantserreetsey

I'd like to hire a snowboard
želim unajmiti snowboard
zheleem oonaymeetee snowboard

they're too big/small
prevelike/premale su
prreveleekey/prremaley soo

a day pass
dnevna propusnica
dnevna prropoosneetsa

I'm a complete beginner
ja sam totalni početnik *(m)*/totalna početnica *(f)*
ya sam totalnee pochetneek/totalna pochetneetsa

Understanding

propusnica za žičaru	lift pass
sedežnica	chair lift
skijaška žičara	ski lift
vlečnica, sidro	T-bar, button lift

OTHER SPORTS

Expressing yourself

where can we hire bikes?
gdje možemo unajmiti bicikle?
gdyey mozhemo oonaymeetee beetseekley?

are there any cycle paths?
postoje li ovdje biciklističke staze?
postoyey lee ovdyey beetseekleesteechkey stazey?

does anyone have a football?
ima li netko nogometnu loptu?
eema lee netko nogometnoo loptoo?

which team do you support?
za koji klub navijaš?
za koyee kloob naveeyash?

I support …
navijam za …
naveeyam za …

is there an open-air swimming pool?
postoji li ovdje otvoreni bazen?
postoyee lee ovdyey otvorrenee bazen?

I've never been diving before
do sada nikada nisam ronio *(m)*/ronila *(f)*
do sada neekada neesam rroneeo/rroneela

I'd like to take beginners' sailing lessons
želim ići na satove jedrenja za početnike
zheleem eechee na satovey yedrrenya za pochetneekey

I run for half an hour every morning
trčim pola sata svakog jutra
trrcheem pola sata svakog yootrra

what do I do if the kayak capsizes?
što mi je činiti ako se kajak prevrne?
shto mee yey cheeneetee ako sey kayak prrevrrney?

Understanding

ima tenisko igralište, otvoreno za javnost, u blizini kolodvora
there's a public tennis court not far from the station

tenisko igralište je zauzeto
the tennis court's occupied

da li vam je to prvi put da jašete?
is this the first time you've been horse-riding?

znate li plivati?
can you swim?

igrate li košarku?
do you play basketball?

INDOOR GAMES

Expressing yourself

shall we have a game of cards?
hoćemo li odigrati partiju karata?
Hochemo lee odeegratee parrteeyoo karrata?

does anyone know any good card games?
zna li netko neku dobru kartašku igru?
zna lee netko nekoo dobrroo karrtashkoo eegrroo?

is anyone up for a game of Monopoly®?
hoće li netko igrati Monopoly?
Hochey lee netko eegrrateee monopoly?

it's your turn
ti si/vi ste na redu
tee see/vee stey na rredoo

Understanding

znate li igrati šah?
do you know how to play chess?

imate li karte?
do you have a pack of cards?

Some informal epressions

posve sam izmožden/izmoždena I'm absolutely knackered
slistio me je he totally thrashed me

| **SHOPPING** | |

Shops are open from 7am to 8pm, Monday to Saturday. Most shops are open until 12 noon or 1pm on Sundays.

A small grocery shop is known as **dućan** or **trgovina**. These shops sell basic foodstuffs (including fresh produce and bread) and household goods. They generally only accept cash.

A larger store is called **robna kuća**. Such stores sell food and also clothes and other goods. Most take credit cards.

You can buy cigarettes from newspaper kiosks (**kiosk** or **trafika**), found on almost every street corner.

Clothing and shoe sizes are the same as in the rest of Europe.

Some informal expressions
to je čista pljačka! that's a rip-off!
švorc sam, dekintiran sam I'm skint
košta k'o svetog Petra kajgana it costs an arm and a leg
to je bagatela it's a real bargain
cijena su drastično pale prices slashed

The basics

bakery	pekara *pekarra*
butcher's	mesnica *mesneetsa*
cash desk	blagajna *blagayna*
cheap	jeftino *yefteeno*
checkout	blagajna *blagayna*
clothes	odjeća *odyecha*
department store	robna kuća *rrobna koocha*
expensive	skupo *skoopo*

gram	gram *grram*
greengrocer's	voćarnica *vocharrneetsa*
hypermarket	supermarket *sooperrmarrket*
kilo	kilogram *keelogrram*
present	poklon *poklon*
price	cijena *tseeyena*
receipt	račun *rrachoon*
refund	naknada *naknada*
sales	rasprodaja *rrasprrodaya*
sales assistant	trgovački pomoćnik *(m)*/trgovačka pomoćnica *(f)* *trrgovachkee pomochneek/ trrgovachka pomochneetsa*
shop	dućan *doochan*
shopping centre	trgovački centar *trrgovachkee tsentarr*
souvenir	suvenir *sooveneerr*
supermarket	samoposluživanje *samoposloozheevanyey*
to buy	kupovati *koopovatee*
to cost	stajati *stayatee*
to pay	platiti *plateetee*
to sell	prodati *prrodatee*

Expressing yourself

is there a supermarket near here?
ima li samoposluživanje u blizini?
ima lee samoposloozheevanyey oo bleezeenee?

where can I buy cigarettes?	**I'd like …**
gdje mogu kupiti cigarete?	želim …
gdyey mogoo koopeetee tseegarretey?	*zheleem …*

I'm looking for …	**do you sell …?**
tražim …	prodajete li …?
trrazheem …	*prrodayetey lee …?*

do you know where I might find some …?
znate li gdje mogu naći …?
znatey lee gdyey mogoo nachee …?

can you order it for me?
možete li to naručiti za mene?
mozhetey lee to narroocheetee za meney?

how much is this?
koliko ovo stoji?
koleeko ovo stoyee?

I'll take it
uzet ću
oozet choo

I haven't got much money
nemam puno novaca
nemam poono novatsa

I haven't got enough money
nemam dovoljno novaca
nemam dovolyno novatsa

that's everything, thanks
to je sve, hvala
to yey svey, Hvala

can I have a (plastic) bag?
mogu li dobiti vrećicu?
mogoo lee dobeetee vrrecheetsoo?

I think you've made a mistake with my change
mislim da mi niste točno uzvratili novac
meesleem da mee neestey tochno oozvrrateelee novats

SHOPPING

Understanding

otvoreno od … do …	open from … to …
rasprodaje	sales
specijalne ponude	special offer
zatvoreno nedjeljom od 13.00 do 15.00 sati	closed Sundays/1pm to 3pm

želite još nešto?
will there be anything else?

želite li vrećicu?
would you like a bag?

PAYING

Expressing yourself

where do I pay?
gdje mogu platiti?
gdyey mogoo plateetee?

how much do I owe you?
koliko vam dugujem?
koleeko vam doogooyem?

could you write it down for me, please?
možete li mi to napisati, molim vas?
mozhetey lee mee to napeesatee, moleem vas?

can I pay by credit card?
mogu li platiti kreditnom karticom?
mogoo lee plateetee krredeetnom karrteetsom?

I'll pay in cash
plaćam gotovinom
placham gotoveenom

I'm sorry, I haven't got any change
žao mi je, nemam ništa sitnog
zhao mee yey, nemam neeshta seetnog

can I have a receipt?
mogu li dobiti račun?
mogoo lee dobeetee rrachoon?

Understanding

plaćate na blagajni
pay at the cash desk

kako želite platiti?
how would you like to pay?

imate li nešto sitnije?
do you have anything smaller?

imate li ikakav dokument uz sebe?
have you got any ID?

potpišite ovdje, molim vas
could you sign here, please?

FOOD

Expressing yourself

where can I buy food around here?
gdje, u blizini, mogu kupiti hranu?
gdyey, oo bleezeenee, mogoo koopeetee Hrranoo?

is there a market nearby?
ima li tržnica u blizini?
ima lee trrzhneetsa oo bleezeenee?

is there a bakery around here?
ima li pekara u blizini?
eema lee pekarra oo bleezeenee?

I'm looking for the cereal aisle
tražim police sa žitnim pahuljicama
trrazheem poleetsey sa zheetneem paHoolyeetsama

I'd like five slices of ham
želim pet kriški šunke
zheleem pet krreeshkee shoonkey

I'd like some of that goat's cheese
želim malo tog kozjeg sira
zheleem malo tog kozyeg seerra

it's for four people
to je za četiri osobe
to yey za cheteeree osobey

about 300 grams
oko 300 grama
oko trreesto grrama

a kilo of apples, please
kilogram jabuka, molim vas
keelogrram yabooka, moleem vas

a bit less/more
malo manje/više
malo manyey/veeshey

can I taste it?
smijem li kušati?
smeeyem lee kooshatee?

does it travel well?
može li izdržati putovanje?
mozhey lee eezdrrzhatee pootovanyey?

Understanding

delikates ni dućan — delicatessen
domaće — homemade
domaći specijaliteti — local specialities
organsko — organic
rok valjanosti … — best before …

tržnica radi svakog dana do 13.00 sati
there's a market every day until 1pm

postoji dućan točno na uglu i otvorena je do kasnih sati
there's a grocer's just on the corner that's open late

CLOTHES

Expressing yourself

I'm looking for the menswear section
tražim odjel muške odjeće
trazheem odyel mooshkey odyechey

no thanks, I'm just looking
ne hvala, samo razgledavam
ney Hvala, samo rrazgledavam

can I try it on?
mogu li probati?
mogoo lee prrobatee?

I'd like to try the one in the window
želim probati ono iz izloga
zheleem prrobatee ono eez eezloga

I take a size 39 *(in shoes)*
nosim cipele broj 39
noseem tseepeley brroy trreedeset devet

where are the changing rooms?
gdje se nalaze kabine?
gdyey sey nalazey kabeeney?

it doesn't fit
ne pristaje mi
ney prreestayey mee

it's too big/small
preveliko/premalo je
prreveleeko/prremalo yey

do you have it in another colour?
imate li neku drugu boju?
eematey lee nekoo drroogoo boyoo?

do you have it in a smaller/bigger size?
imate li manji/veći broj?
eematey lee manyee/vechee brroy?

do you have them in red?
imate li ih u crvenoj boji?
eematey lee eeH oo tsrrvenoy boyee?

yes, that's fine, I'll take them
odgovaraju mi, uzet ću ih
odgovarrayoo mee, oozet choo eeH

no, I don't like it	**I'll think about it**
ne sviđa mi se	malo ću razmisliti
ne sveeja mee sey	*malo choo razmeesleetee*

I'd like to return this, it doesn't fit
želim ovo vratiti, ne odgovara mi
zheleem ovo vrrateetee, ney odgovarra mee

this has a hole in it, can I get a refund?
ima rupu, možete li mi vratiti novac?
eema rroopoo, mozhetey lee mee vrrateetee novats?

Understanding

dječja odjeća	children's clothes
kabine za presvlačenje	changing rooms
muška odjeća	menswear
otvoreno nedjeljom	open Sunday
rublje	lingerie
stvari na rasprodaji ne mogu se vraćati	sale items cannot be returned
ženska odjeća	ladieswear

| **bok, mogu li vam pomoći?** | **imamo samo u plavoj i crnoj boji** |
| hello, can I help you? | we only have it in blue or black |

| **nemamo više ništa te veličine** | **pristaje vam** |
| we don't have any left in that size | it suits you |

| **dobro pristaje** | **možete vratiti ako vam ne pristaje** |
| it's a good fit | you can bring it back if it doesn't fit |

SOUVENIRS AND PRESENTS

Expressing yourself

I'm looking for a present to take home
tražim dar za ponijeti kući
trrazheem darr za poneeyetee koochee

I'd like something that's easy to transport
želim nešto što se jednostavno može transportirati
zheleem neshto shto se yednostavno mozhey trransporrteerratee

it's for a little girl of four
to je za četverogodišnju djevojčicu
to yey za chetverrogodeeshnyoo dyevoycheetsoo

could you gift-wrap it for me?
možete li mi to zamotati kao dar, molim vas?
mozhetey lee mee to zamotatee kao darr, moleem vas?

Understanding

izrađeno od drveta/srebra/zlata/vune	made of wood/silver/gold/wool
proizvod izrađen na tradicionalni način	traditionally made product
ručna izrada	handmade
koliko želite potrošiti? how much do you want to spend?	**da li je to dar?** is it for a present?
to je tipično za ovaj kraj it's typical of the region	

PHOTOS	

The basics

black and white	crno-bijelo *tsrrno-beeyelo*
camera	fotoaparat *fotoaparrat*
colour	boja *boya*
copy	kopija *kopeeya*
digital camera	digitalna kamera *deegeetalna kamerra*
disposable camera	fotoaparat za jednokratnu uporabu *fotoaparrat za yednokrratnoo ooporraboo*
exposure	ekspozicija *ekspozeetseeya*
film	film *feelm*
flash	bljeskalica *blyeskaleetsa*, fleš *flesh*
glossy	sjajan *syayan*
matte	mat *mat*
memory card	memorijska kartica *memoreeyska karrteetsa*
negative	negativ *negateev*
passport photo	fotografija za putovnicu *fotogrrafeeya za pootovneetsoo*
photo booth	automat za fotografiranje *aootomat za fotogrrafeerranyey*
reprint	pretisak *prreteesak*
slide	dijapozitiv *deeyapozeeteev*
to get photos developed	razviti fotografije *rrazveetee fotogrrafeeyey*
to take a photo/photos	fotografirati *fotogrrafeerratee*

Expressing yourself

could you take a photo of us, please?
možete li nas fotografirati, molim vas?
mozhetey lee nas fotogrrafeerratee, moleem vas?

you just have to press this button
samo pritisnete ovo dugme
samo prreeteesnetey ovo doogmey

I'd like a 200 ASA colour film
želim film u boji od 200ASA
zheleem feelm oo boyee od dvjesto ASA

do you have black and white films?
imate li crno-bijele filmove?
eematey lee tsrrno-beeyeley feelmovey?

how much is it to develop a film of 36 photos?
koliko stoji razvijanje filma od 36 snimki?
koleeko stoyee rrazveeyanyey feelma od trreedeset shest sneemkee?

I'd like to have this film developed
želim razviti ovaj film
zheleem rrazveetee ovay feelm

I'd like extra copies of some of the photos
od nekih fotografija želim više kopija
od nekeeH fotogrrafeeya zheleem veeshey kopeeya

three copies of this one and two of this one
tri kopije od ove i dvije od ove
trree kopeeyey od ovey ee dveeyey od ovey

can I print my digital photos here?
mogu li ovdje otiskati digitalne fotografije?
mogoo lee ovdyey oteeskatey deegeetalney fotogrrafeeyey?

can you put these photos on a CD for me?
možete li mi pospremiti ove fotografije na CD?
mozhetey lee mee posprremeetee ovey fotogrrafeeyey na tsey dey?

I've come to pick up my photos
došao *(m)*/došla *(f)* sam po fotografije
doshao/doshla sam po fotogrrafeeyey

I've got a problem with my camera
nešto mi nije u redu s fotoaparatom
neshto mee neeyey oo redoo s fotoaparratom

I don't know what it is
ne znam o čemu se radi
ney znam o chemoo sey rradee

the flash doesn't work
bljeskalica ne radi
blyeskaleetsa ney rradee

Understanding

fotografije će biti gotove za sat vremena photos developed in one hour

standardna veličina standard format

ekspresna usluga express service

fotografije na CD-u photos on CD

možda je baterija potrošena
maybe the battery's dead

imamo stroj za tiskanje digitalnih fotografija
we have a machine for printing digital photos

vaše ime, molim vas
what's the name, please?

za kada ih želite?
when do you want them for?

možemo ih razviti za sat vremena
we can develop them in an hour

fotografije će vam biti gotove u četvrtak u podne
your photos will be ready on Thursday at noon

BANKS €

The Croatian currency is the **kuna**, which is divided into 100 **lipa**. In big cities, banks are open from 7am to 7pm Monday to Friday, and from 7am to 12 or 1pm on Saturdays. In small towns and villages, they are open from 7am to noon, or sometimes 2pm.

Bureaux de change (**mjenjačnica**) can be found throughout the country. They rarely accept travellers cheques or bank cards. Their exchange rates are similar to those in banks.

Cards are accepted in most shops, restaurants and hotels in big cities. Cash dispensers are easy to find in towns and the tourist areas of the Dalmatian coast. They take most credit cards. Note that on many cash machines it is possible to change the display language.

Travellers cheques are accepted in all banks, but the exchange rate is much less favourable than for cash.

The basics

bank	banka *banka*
bank account	bankovni račun *bankovnee rachoon*
banknote	novčanica *novchaneetsa*
bureau de change	mjenjačnica *myenyachneetsa*
cashpoint	bankomat *bankomat*
change	sitniš *seetneesh*
cheque	ček *chek*
coin	kovanica *kovaneetsa*
commission	provizija *prroveezeeya*
credit card	kreditna kartica *krredeetna karrteetsa*
money	novac *novats*
PIN (number)	PIN *peen*
transfer	prijenos *prreeyenos*
Travellers Cheques®	putnički čekovi *pootneechkee chekovee*
withdrawal	podizanje *podeezanyey*
to change	usitniti *ooseetneetee*

to withdraw   podizati *podeezatee*

Expressing yourself

where I can get some money changed?
gdje mogu promijeniti novac?
gdyey mogoo prromeeyeneetee novats?

are banks open on Saturdays?
rade li banke subotom?
rradey lee bankey soobotom?

I'm looking for a cashpoint
tražim bankomat
trrazheem bankomat

I'd like to change £100
želim promijeniti 100 funti
zheleem prromeeyeneetee sto foontee

what commission do you charge?
kakva vam je provizija?
kakva vam yey prroveezeeya?

I'd like to transfer some money
želim doznačiti novac
zheleem doznacheetee novats

I'd like to report the loss of my credit card
želim prijaviti gubitak kreditne kartice
zheleem prreeyaveetee goobeetak krredeetney karteetsey

the cashpoint has swallowed my card
bankomat mi je progutao karticu
bankomat mee yey prrogootao karrteetsoo

Understanding

molim ubacite karticu
please insert your card

utipkajte vaš pin
please enter your PIN number

molim odaberite sumu za podizanje
please select amount for withdrawal

podizanje s potvrdom
withdrawal with receipt

podizanje bez potvrde
withdrawal without receipt

molim, odaberite sumu koju želite
please select the amount you require

u kvaru
out of service

Some informal expressions

lova money
perje money

POST OFFICES

Post offices in Croatia have an **HP** sign and can be found even in small villages. They are open from 7am to 7pm during the week (but only until 2pm in rural areas), and from 7am to noon on Saturdays. In big cities and tourist areas, opening hours are usually longer in high season, with many post offices staying open until 9pm and on Sunday mornings.

Post offices sell stamps, and also allow you to change money and make Western Union transfers. They also have public telephones.

Letter boxes are yellow, and there are plenty of them. There are separate slots for local mail (**unutrašnji promet**) and international mail (**međunarodni promet**). It usually takes at least ten days for a postcard and five days for a letter to reach the UK.

The basics

airmail	zrakoplovom *zrrakoplovom*
envelope	kuverta *kooverrta*
letter	pismo *peesmo*
mail	poštanske pošiljke *poshtanskey posheelkey*
parcel	paket *paket*
post	pošta *poshta*
postbox	poštanski sandučić *poshtanskee sandoocheech*
postcard	poštanska dopisnica *poshtanska dopeesneetsa*, razglednica *rrazgledneetsa*
postcode	poštanski broj *poshtanskee brroy*
post office	pošta *poshta*
stamp	poštanska marka *poshtanska marrka*
to post	poslati *poslatee*
to send	poslati *poslatee*
to write	pisati *peesatee*

Expressing yourself

is there a post office around here?
da li je u blizini pošta?
da lee yey oo bleezeenee poshta?

is there a postbox near here?
da li je u blizini poštanski sandučić?
da lee yey oo bleezeenee poshtanskee sandoocheech?

is the post office open on Saturdays?
radi li pošta subotom?
rradee lee poshta soobotom?

what time does the post office close?
kada se zatvara pošta?
kada sey zatvarra poshta?

I'd like ... stamps for the UK, please
želim ... poštanskih maraka za Veliku Britaniju, molim vas
zheleem ... poshtanskeeH marraka za Veleekoo Brreetaneeyoo, moleem vas

how long will it take to arrive?
koliko će dugo putovati?
koleeko che doogo pootovatee?

where can I buy envelopes?
gdje mogu kupiti kuverte?
gdyey mogoo koopeetee kooverrtey?

do you sell stamps?
prodajete li poštanske marke?
prrodayetey lee poshtanskey marrkey?

is there any post for me?
ima li pošte za mene?
eema lee poshtey za meney?

Understanding

lomljivo	fragile
oprezno rukovati	handle with care
posljednja otprema	last collection
pošiljatelj	sender
prva otprema	first collection

trajat će od tri do pet dana
it'll take between three and five days

INTERNET CAFÉS AND E-MAIL

There are more and more Internet cafés in Croatia, and you will find them in all the big towns. As Internet usage becomes more widespread, it is becoming more common to swap e-mail addresses with people.

Almost all computers in Croatia run on English-language operating systems and have QWERTY keyboards. Even in Croatian, many computer terms are borrowed from English as you will see in this chapter.

The basics

at sign	monkey znak *monkey znak*
e-mail	elektronska pošta *elektrronska poshta*
e-mail address	e-mail adresa *e-mail adrresa*
Internet café	Internet cafe *eenterrnet kafey*
key	tipka *teepka*
keyboard	tipkovnica *teepkovneetsa*
to copy	kopirati *kopeerratee*
to cut	izrezati *eezrrezatee*
to delete	obrisati *obrreesatee*
to download	preuzimati podatke *prreoozeematee podatkey*
to e-mail somebody	poslati nekome e-mail *poslatee nekomey e-mail*
to paste	zalijepiti *zaleeyepeetee*
to receive	primati *preematee*
to save	sačuvati *sachoovatee*
to send an e-mail	poslati e-mail *poslatee e-mail*

Expressing yourself

is there an Internet café near here?
ima li Internet cafe u blizini?
eema lee eenterrnet kafey oo bleezeenee?

how do I get online?
kako idem online?
kako eedem online?

do you have an e-mail address?
imaš li e-mail adresu?
eemash lee e-mail adrresoo?

I'd just like to check my e-mails
samo želim provjeriti elektronsku poštu
samo zheleem prrovyerreetee elektrronskoo poshtoo

would you mind helping me, I'm not sure what to do
možete li mi pomoći, nisam siguran *(m)*/sigurna *(f)* što trebam učiniti
mozhetey lee mee pomochee, neesam seegoorran/seegoorrna shto trrebam oocheeneetee

I can't find the at sign on this keyboard
ne mogu pronaći monkey znak na ovoj tipkovnici
ney mogoo prronachee monkey znak na ovoy teepkovneetsee

when do I pay?
kada se plaća?
kada sey placha?

it's not working
ne radi
ney rradee

there's something wrong with the computer, it's frozen
nešto nije u redu s kompjuterom, zamrznuo se
nehsto neeyey oo rredoo s kompyooterrom, zamrznooo sey

how much will it be for half an hour?
koja je cijena za pola sata?
koya yey tseeyena za pola sata?

Understanding

ulazni pretinac	inbox
izlazni pretinac	outbox

morat ćete pričekati dvadesetak minuta
you'll have to wait for 20 minutes or so

samo pitajte ako niste sigurni što trebate učiniti
just ask if you're not sure what to do

utipkajte ovu lozinku i ulogirat ćete se
just enter this password to log on

| **TELEPHONE** | |

The use of mobile phones is widespread, and they work in most areas (except in some mountain regions where it may be impossible to receive a signal or reception may be poor). Your UK mobile phone will work on one of the Croatian networks.

Should you not have a mobile, you can make phone calls from public phone boxes or post offices. You will need to buy a phonecard (**telefonska kartica**) from the post office or a newspaper kiosk. Most phone boxes take incoming calls so you can be rung back – the number is printed above the keypad. It's cheaper to phone from a post office. There is no need to queue at the counter: just go straight to the phones and pay when you leave, stating the number of the booth you used. If you want to make several phone calls in a row, don't hang up – just press the button quickly to get the dial tone again.

Phone numbers are read out one digit at a time. Zero is pronounced **nula**.

To call the UK from Croatia, dial 00 44 followed by the phone number, including the area code but omitting the first zero. The international dialling code for Ireland is 00 353, and for the US and Canada it is 001.

To call Croatia from abroad, dial 00 385 followed by the area code and number, omitting the first zero.

For calls within Croatia, you will need to use the area code unless you are already in that area. The area code corresponds to the first two digits of the postcode: 01 for Zagreb and the suburbs, 031 for Osijek and Slavonia, 051 for Rijeka and Kvarner, 052 for Pula and Istria, 023 for the Zadar region, 022 for Šibenik, 021 for Split and Central Dalmatia and 020 for Dubrovnik and Southern Dalmatia.

The basics

answering machine	automatska sekretarica *aootomatska sekrretarreetsa*
call	poziv *pozeev*
directory enquiries	služba informacija *sloozhba eenforrmatseeya*
hello	halo *Halo*
international call	međunarodni poziv *mejoonarrodnee pozeev*
local call	lokalni poziv *lokalnee pozeev*
message	poruka *porrooka*
mobile	mobitel *mobeetel*
national call	tuzemni poziv *toozemnee pozeev*
phone	telefon *telefon*
phone book	telefonski imenik *telefonskee eemeneek*
phone box	telefonska govornica *telefonska govorrneetsa*
phone call	telefonski poziv *telefonskee pozeev*
phonecard	telefonska kartica *telefonska karrteetsa*
phone number	telefonski broj *telefonskee brroy*
ringtone	zvuk telefonskog zvona *zvook telefonskog zvona*
top-up card	bon za mobitel *bon za mobeetel*
Yellow Pages®	žute stranice *zhootey strraneetsey*
to call somebody	nazvati nekoga *nazvatee nekoga*

Expressing yourself

where can I buy a phonecard?
gdje mogu kupiti telefonsku karticu?
gdyey mogoo koopeetee telefonskoo karrteetsoo?

a ...-kuna top-up card, please
bon za mobitel od ... kuna, molim vas
bon za mobeetel od ... koona, moleem vas

I'd like to make a reverse-charge call
želim nazvati nekoga na njegov trošak
zheleem nazvatee nekoga na nyegov trroshak

is there a phone box near here, please?
molim vas, gdje je telefonska govornica?
moleem vas, gdyey yey telefonska govorrneetsa?

can I plug my phone in here to recharge it?
mogu li uključiti svoj telefon ovdje kako bi se napunio?
mogoo lee ooklyoocheetee svoy telefon ovdyey kako bee sey napooneeo?

do you have a mobile number?
koji je broj vašeg mobitela?
koyee yey brroy vasheg mobeetela?

where can I contact you?
kako vas mogu kontaktirati?
kako vas mogoo kontakteerratee?

did you get my message?
jeste li primili moju poruku?
yestey lee prreemeelee mojoo porrookoo?

Understanding

birali ste nepostojeći broj
the number you have dialled has not been recognized

molim vas pritisnite ljestve
please press the hash key

MAKING A CALL

Expressing yourself

hello, this is David Brown (speaking)
halo, pri telefonu David Brown
Halo, prree telefonoo David Brown

hello, could I speak to ..., please?
mogu li razgovarati s ..., molim vas?
mogoo lee rrazgovarratee s ..., moleem vas?

hello, is that Caroline?
halo, je li to Caroline?
Halo, yey lee to Karrolayn?

do you speak English?
govorite li engleski?
govorreetey lee engleskee?

could you speak more slowly, please?
možete li govoriti polaganije, molim vas?
mozhetey lee govorreetey polaganeeyey, moleem vas?

I can't hear you, could you speak up, please?
ništa vas ne čujem, možete li govoriti glasnije, molim vas?
neeshta vas ne chooyem, mozhetey lee govoreetey glasneeyey, moleem vas?

could you tell him/her I called?
možete li mu/joj reći da sam zvao?
mozhetey lee moo/yoy rrechee da sam zvao?

could you ask him/her to call me back?
možete li ga/ju zamoliti da me nazove?
mozhetey lee ga/yoo zamoleetee da me nazovey?

I'll call back later
nazvat ću ponovno kasnije
nazvat choo ponovno kasneeyey

my name is … and my number is …
ime mi je … moj broj telefona je …
eemey mee yey … moy brroy telefona yey …

do you know when he/she might be available?
da li možda znate kada će biti slobodan/slobodna?
da lee mozhda znatey kada chey beetee slobodan/slobodna?

thank you, goodbye
hvala, doviđenja
Hvala, doveejenya

Understanding

tko zove?
who's calling?

pogriješili ste broj
you've got the wrong number

nije trenutno ovdje
he's/she's not here at the moment

reći ću mu/joj da ste zvali
I'll tell him/her you called

pričekajte trenutak
hold on

želite li ostaviti poruku?
do you want to leave a message?

reći ću mu/joj da vas nazove
I'll ask him/her to call you back

sad ću ga/je pozvati
I'll just hand you over to him/her

PROBLEMS

I don't know the code
ne znam pozivni
ney znam pozeevnee

it's engaged
zauzeto je
zaoozeto yey

there's no reply
nitko ne odgovara
neetko ney odgovarra

I can't get a signal
nema signala
nema seegnala

I couldn't get through
nisam mogao *(m)*/mogla *(f)* dobiti vezu
neesam mogao/mogla dobeetee vezoo

I don't have much credit left on my phone
nemam više puno kredita u telefonu
nemam veeshey poono krredeeta oo telefonoo

we're about to get cut off
uskoro će nas prekinuti
ooskorro chey nas prrekeenootee

the reception's really bad
prijam je doista loš
prreeyam yey doeesta losh

Understanding

jedva jedvice vas čujem
I can hardly hear you

linija je jako loša
it's a bad line

Common abbreviations
posao = broj na poslu work (number)
kuća = broj u kući home (number)
mobitel = broj mobitela mobile (number)

Some informal expressions

nazvati nekoga to make a call
spustiti slušalicu nekome to hang up on somebody

In case of emergency, call 94 for the ambulance service (**Služba za hitnu pomoć**).

Alternatively, go to the hospital casualty department (**dežurna bolnica**) if you are in a city, or a medical centre (**dom zdravlja**) or a doctor's surgery (**liječnička ordinacija**) if you are in a small town or a village.

Foreigners are entitled at least to emergency medical care. However, you should ensure that your travel insurance covers medical treatment.

Pharmacies sell only medicines, a few personal hygiene products, baby food and contraceptives.

Tap water is safe to drink throughout the country.

The basics

allergy	alergija *alerrgeeya*
ambulance	vozilo hitne pomoći *vozeelo Heetney pomochee*
aspirin	aspirin *aspeerreen*
blood	krv *krv*
broken	slomljen *slomlyen*
casualty (department)	traumatologija *trraoomatologeeya*
chemist's	ljekarna *lyekarrna*
condom	prezervativ *prrezerrvateev*
dentist	zubar *zoobarr*
diarrhoea	proljev *prrolyev*
doctor	liječnik *leeyechneek*
food poisoning	trovanje hranom *trrovanyey Hrranom*
GP	liječnik opće prakse *leeyechneek opchey prraksey*
gynaecologist	ginekolog *geenekolog*
hospital	bolnica *bolneetsa*

infection	infekcija *eenfektseeya*
medicine	lijek *leeyek*
painkiller	sredstvo protiv bolova *srredstvo prroteev bolova*
period	mjesečnica *myesechneetsa*
plaster	flaster *flasterr*
rash	osip *oseep*
spot	prišt *prreesht*
sunburn	opekline od sunca *opekleeney od soontsa*
surgical spirit	alkohol *alkoHol*
tablet	tableta *tableta*
temperature	temperatura *temperratoorra*
vaccination	cijepljenje *tseeyeplyenyey*
x-ray	rendgen *rrendgen*
to disinfect	dezinficirati *dezeenfeetseerratee*
to faint	onesvijestiti se *onestveeyesteetee sey*
to vomit	povraćati *povrrachatee*

Expressing yourself

does anyone have an aspirin/a tampon/a plaster, by any chance?
ima li itko, slučajno, aspirin/tampon/flaster ?
eema lee eetko, sloochayno, aspeereen/tampon/flasterr?

I need to see a doctor
moram otići liječniku
morram oteechee leeyechneekoo

where can I find a doctor?
gdje mogu pronaći liječnika?
gdyey mogoo prronachee leeyechneeka?

I'd like to make an appointment for today
želim zakazati sastanak za danas
zheleem zakazatee sastanak za danas

as soon as possible
što je moguće prije
shto yey mogoochey prreeyey

no, it doesn't matter
ne, nije važno
ney, neeyey vazhno

can you send an ambulance to …
možete li poslati vozilo hitne pomoći do …
mozhetey lee poslatee vozeelo Heetney pomochee do …

I've broken my glasses
slomile su mi se naočale
slomeeley soo mee sey naochaley

I've lost a contact lens
izgubio *(m)*/izgubila *(f)* sam leće
eezgoobeeo/eezgoobeela sam lechey

Understanding

liječnička ordinacija	doctor's surgery
odjel za traumatologiju	casualty department
recept	prescription

nema slobodnih termina do četvrtak
there are no available appointments until Thursday

da li je petak u 14.00 sati u redu?
is Friday at 2pm ok?

AT THE DOCTOR'S OR THE HOSPITAL

Expressing yourself

I have an appointment with Dr …
imam zakazan pregled kod dr …
eemam zakazan prregled kod drr …

I don't feel very well
ne osjećam se dobro
ney osyecham sey dobrro

I feel very weak
osjećam se jako nemoćno
osyecham sey yako nemochno

I don't know what it is
ne znam što je to
ney znam shto yey to

I've been bitten/stung by …
ugrizao/ubo me je …
oogrreezao/oobo mey yey …

I've got a headache
imam glavobolju
eemam glavobolyoo

I've got toothache/stomachache
boli me zub/trbuh
bolee mey zoob/trrbooH

I've got a sore throat
peče me grlo
pechey mey grrlo

my back hurts
bole me leđa
boley mey leja

it hurts
boli me
bolee mey

it hurts here
ovdje me boli
ovdyey mey bolee

I feel sick
muka mi je
mooka mee yey

it's got worse
pogoršalo se
pogorrshalo sey

it's been three days
prošlo je tri dana
prroshlo yey trree dana

it started last night
počelo je prošle noći
pochelo yey prroshley nochee

it's never happened to me before
nikada mi se to ranije nije dogodilo
neekada mee sey to rraneeyey neeyey dogodeelo

I've got a temperature
imam vrućicu/povišenu temperaturu
eemam vrroocheetsoo/poveeshenoo temperratoorroo

I have asthma
bolujem od astme
bolooyem od astmey

I have a heart condition
imam srčanih tegoba
eemam srrchaneeH tegoba

I've been on antibiotics for a week and I'm not getting any better
već sam tjedan dana na antibioticima i nije mi ništa bolje
vech sam tyedan dana na anteebeeoteetseema ee neeyey mee neeshta bolyey

it itches
svrbi me
svrrbee mey

I'm on the pill/the minipill
uzimam pilulu/mini pilulu
oozeemam peelooloo/meenee peelooloo

I'm ... months pregnant
trudna sam ... mjeseci
trroodna sam ... myesetsee

I'm allergic to penicillin
alergičan *(m)*/alergična *(f)* sam na penicilin
alerrgeechan/alerrgeechna sam na peneetseeleen

I've twisted my ankle
uganuo *(m)*/uganula *(f)* sam gležanj
ooganuo/ooganoola sam glezhany

I fell and hurt my back
pao (m)/pala (f) sam i povrijedio (m)/povrijedila (f) kralježnicu
pao/pala sam ee povrreeyedeeo/povrreeyedeela kralyezhneetsoo

I've had a blackout
privremeno sam izgubio (m)/izgubila (f) svijest
prreevrremeno sam eezgoobeeo/eezgoobeela sveeyest

I've lost a filling
pala mi je plomba
pala mee yey plomba

is it serious?
je li to ozbiljno?
yey lee to ozbeelno?

is it contagious?
je li zarazno?
yey lee zarrazno?

how is he/she?
kako mu/joj je?
kako moo/yoy yey?

how much do I owe you?
koliko vam dugujem?
koleeko vam doogooyem?

can I have a receipt so I can get the money refunded?
mogu li dobiti priznanicu kako bih zatražio (m)/zatražila (f) povrat novca?
mogoo lee dobeetee prreeznaneetsoo kako beeH zatrrazheeo/zatrrazheela povrrat novtsa?

Understanding

pričekajte u čekaonici, molim vas
if you'd like to take a seat in the waiting room

gdje vas boli?
where does it hurt?

duboko udahnite
take a deep breath

ispružite se, molim vas
lie down, please

da li vas boli kad pritisnem ovdje?
does it hurt when I press here?

da li ste cijepljeni protiv ...?
have you been vaccinated against …?

da li ste alergični na ...?
are you allergic to …?

uzimate li bilo kakve druge lijekove?
are you taking any other medication?

napisat ću vam recept
I'm going to write you a prescription

trebalo bi proći za nekoliko dana
it should clear up in a few days

trebalo bi brzo zarasti
it should heal quickly

morat ćemo vas operirati
you're going to need an operation

dođite na kontrolni pregled za tjedan dana
come back and see me in a week

AT THE CHEMIST'S

Expressing yourself

I'd like a box of plasters, please
molim vas kutiju flastera
*moleem vas koo*tee*yoo fla*sterra

could I have something for a bad cold?
mogu li dobiti nešto za doista jaku prehladu?
mogoo lee dobeetee neshto za doeesta yakoo prreHladoo?

I need something for a cough
treba mi nešto protiv kašlja
trreba mee neshto prroteev kashlya

I'm allergic to aspirin
alergičan *(m)*/alergična *(f)* sam na aspirine
alerrgeechan/alerrgeechna sam na aspeerreeney

I need the morning-after pill
trebam pilulu za dan poslije
trrebam peelooloo za dan posleeyey

I'd like to try a homeopathic remedy
želim iskušati homeopatski lijek
zheleem eeskooshatee Homeopatskee leeyek

I'd like a bottle of solution for soft contact lenses
treba mi boca otopine za mekane kontaktne leće
treba mee botsa otopeeney za mekaney kontaktney lechey

Understanding

čepići	suppositories
izdaje se samo na liječnički recept	available on prescription only
kapsule	capsules
kontraindikacije	contra-indications
krema	cream
mast	ointment
moguće nuspojave	possible side effects
prah	powder
primijeniti	apply
sirup	syrup
tableta	tablet
uzimajte tri puta dnevno prije jela	take three times a day before meals

---

Some informal expressions

biti prikovan za krevet to be stuck in bed
osjećati se jadno to feel rough
imati prehladu stoljeća to have a stinking cold
pasti u afan to pass out
kurton condom

PROBLEMS AND EMERGENCIES

(i)

If you get lost in a city, don't hesitate to ask for help at hotel receptions or in local shops, or ask a police officer (**POLICAJAC**).

In a road accident, you must contact the traffic police to make your statement.

Some useful phone numbers are as follows: the police (**policija**) is 92, the fire brigade (**vatrogasci**) is 93, medical emergencies (**hitna medicinska pomoć**) is 94. The car breakdown service (**pomoć na cesti**) is 987 and the emergency and information centre (**centar za obavješćivanje**) is 985

The basics

accident	nezgoda *nezgoda*
ambulance	vozilo hitne pomoći *vozeelo Heetney pomochee*
broken	slomljen *slomlyen*
coastguard	obalna straža *obalna strrazha*
disabled person	invalidna osoba *eenvaleedna osoba*
doctor	liječnik *leeyechneek*
emergency	hitan slučaj *Heetan sloochay*
fire brigade	vatrogasci *vatrrogastsee*
fire	požar *pozharr*
hospital	bolnica *bolneetsa*
ill	bolestan *bolestan*
injured	ozlijeđen *ozleeyejen*
late	kasni *kasnee*
police	policija *poleetseeya*

Expressing yourself

can you help me?
možete li mi pomoći?
mozhetey lee mee pomochee?

help!
u-pomoć!
oo-pomoch!

fire!
požar!
pozharr!

be careful!
budi oprezan!
boodee oprrezan!

it's an emergency!
to je hitan slučaj!
to yey Heetan sloochay!

could I borrow your phone, please?
mogu li posuditi vaš telefon, molim vas?
mogoo lee posoodeetee vash telefon, moleem vas?

there's been an accident
dogodila se nezgoda
dogodeela sey nezgoda

does anyone here speak English?
da li netko ovdje govori engleski?
da lee netko ovdyey govorree engleskee?

I need to contact the British consulate
moram stupiti u vezu s britanskim poslanstvom
morram stoopeetee oo vezoo s brreetanskim poslanstvom

where's the nearest police station?
gdje je najbliža policijska postaja?
gdyey yey naybleezha poleetseeyska postaya?

what do I have to do?
što trebam učiniti?
shto trrebam oocheeneetee?

my passport/credit card has been stolen
ukradena mi je putovnica/kreditna kartica
ookrradena mee yey pootovneetsa/krredeetna karrteetsa

PROBLEMS, EMERGENCIES

my bag's been snatched
oteta mi je torbica
oteta mee yey torrbeetsa

I've been attacked
napadnut sam
napadnoot sam

my car's been towed away
pauk mi je odnio auto
paook mee yey odneeo aooto

my car's been broken into
netko mi je provalio u auto
netko mee yey prrovaleeo oo aooto

there's a man following me
slijedi me neki čovjek
sleeyedee mey nekee chovyek

is there disabled access?
postoji li pristup za invalide?
postoyee lee prreestoop za eenvaleedey?

he's drowning, get help!
utapa se, pozovite pomoć!
ootapa sey, pozoveetey pomoch!

can you keep an eye on my things for a minute?
možete li mi na trenutak pričuvati stvari?
mozhetey lee mee na trrenootak prreechoovatee stvarree?

I've lost …
izgubio (m)/izgubila (f) sam …
eezgoobeeo/eezgoobeela sam …

my son/daughter is missing
nestao/nestala mi je sin/kćer
nestao/nestala mee yey seen/kcherr

I've broken down
pokvario mi se auto
pokvarreeo mee sey aooto

Understanding

dežurna policijska služba	police emergency services
gorska služba spašavanja	mountain rescue
izgubljeno-nađeno	lost property
izlaz u slučaju nužde	emergency exit
pomoć na cestama	breakdown service
pozor, oštar pas!	beware of the dog
u kvaru	out of order

POLICE

Expressing yourself

I want to report something stolen
želim prijaviti krađu
zheleem prreeyaveetee krrajoo

I need a document from the police for my insurance company
potrebna mi je policijska potvrda za osiguravajuće društvo
potrrebna mee yey poleetseeyska potvrrda za oseegoorravayoochey drrooshtvo

Understanding

Filling in forms

prezime	surname
ime	first name
adresa	address
poštanski broj	postcode
zemlja	country
nacionalnost	nationality
datum rođenja	date of birth
mjesto rođenja	place of birth
dob	age
spol	sex
trajanje boravka	duration of stay
datum dolaska/odlaska	arrival/departure date
zanimanje	occupation
broj putovnice	passport number

na ovu se stvar plaća carina
there's customs duty to pay on this item

možete li otvoriti ovu torbu, molim vas?
would you open this bag, please?

što nedostaje?
what's missing?

kada se to dogodilo?
when did this happen?

gdje ste odsjeli?
where are you staying?

možete li ga/je opisati?
can you describe him/her/it?

možete li ispuniti ovaj formular, molim vas?
would you fill in this form, please?

možete li ovdje potpisati, molim vas?
would you sign here, please?

Some informal expressions

murjak cop
tat slammer, nick
biti oplindran to get nicked
nešto mi je maznuto to get something nicked

The basics

after	poslije *posleeyey*
already	već *vech*
always	uvijek *ooveeyek*
at lunchtime	oko ručka *oko roochka*
at the beginning/end of	na početku/na kraju *na pochetkoo/na krrayoo*
at the moment	u ovom trenutku *oo ovom trrenootkoo*
before	prije *prreeyey*
between ... and ...	između ... i ... *eezmejoo ... ee ...*
day	dan *dan*
during	tijekom *teeyekom* (+ gen)
early	rano *rrano*
evening	večer *vecherr*
for a long time	dugo vremena *doogo vrremena*
from ... to ...	od ...do ... *od ... do ...*
from time to time	s vremena na vrijeme *s vrremena na vrreeyemey*
in a little while	za koji trenutak *za koyee trrenootak*
in the evening	navečer *navecherr*
in the middle of	usred *oosrred* (+ gen)
last	posljednji *poslyednyee*
late	kasno *kasno*
midday	podne *podney*
midnight	ponoć *ponoch*
morning	jutro *yootrro*
month	mjesec *myesets*
never	nikada *neekada*
next	sljedeći *slyedechee*
night	noć *noch*
not yet	ne još *ney yosh*
now	sada *sada*
occasionally	povremeno *povrremeno*
often	često *chesto*
rarely	rijetko *rreeyetko*

recently	nedavno *nedavno*
since	od *od* (+ gen)
sometimes	ponekad *ponekad*
soon	uskoro *ooskorro*
still	još uvijek *josh ooveeyek*
straightaway	odmah *odmaH*
until	sve do *svey do* (+ gen)
week	tjedan *tyedan*
weekend	vikend *veekend*
year	godina *godeena*

Expressing yourself

see you soon!
do skorog viđenja!
do skorrog veejenya!

see you later!
doviđenja!
doveejenya!

see you on Monday!
vidimo se u ponedjeljak!
veedeemo sey oo ponedyelyak!

have a good weekend!
želim ti ugodan vikend!
zheleem tee oogodan veekend!

sorry I'm late
ispričavam se što kasnim
eesprreechavam sey shto kasneem

I haven't been there yet
još nisam bio *(m)*/bila *(f)* tamo
yosh neesam beeo/beela tamo

I haven't had time to
nisam imao *(m)*/imala *(f)* vremena
neesam eemao/eemala vrremena

I've got plenty of time
imam vremena na pretek
eemam vrremena na prretek

I'm in a rush
u žurbi sam
oo zhoorrbee sam

hurry up!
požuri *(sg)*/požurite *(pl)*!
pozhooree/pozhooreetey!

just a minute, please
samo trenutak, molim vas
samo treenootak, moleem vas

I had a late night
kasno sam zaspao *(m)*/zaspala *(f)*
kasno sam zaspao/zaspala

I got up early
rano sam ustao *(m)*/ustala *(f)*
rrano sam oostao/oostala

I waited ages
dugo sam čekao *(m)*/čekala *(f)*
doogo sam chekao/chekala

TIME AND DATE

I have to get up very early tomorrow to catch my plane
moram sutra ustati jako rano, jer mi polijeće zrakoplov
morram sootrra oostatee yako rrano yerr mee poleeyechey zrrakoplov

we only have four days left
imamo još samo četiri dana
eemamo yosh samo cheteerree dana

THE DATE

How to express dates:

5 July 2006	5. srpanj 2006. godine (godine = in the year)
in the 21st century	XXI stoljeće (dvadeset i prvo stoljeće)
19th-century art	umjetnost XIX stoljeća (umjetnost devetnaestog stoljeća)

The basics

... ago	... prije *prreeyey* ...
at the beginning/end of	na početku/na kraju *na pochetkoo/na krrayoo*
in the middle of	u sredini *oo srredeenee* (+ gen)
in two days' time	za dva dana *za dva dana*
last night	prošle noći *prroshley nochee*
the day after tomorrow	preksutra *prreksootrra*
the day before yesterday	prekjučer *prrekyoocherr*
today	danas *danas*
tomorrow	sutra *sootrra*
tomorrow morning/ afternoon/evening	sutra ujutro/poslijepodne/navečer *sootra ooyootrro/posleeyepodney/navecherr*
yesterday	jučer *yoocherr*
yesterday morning/ afternoon/evening	jučer ujutro/poslijepodne/navečer *yoocherr ooyootrro/posleeyepodney/navecherr*

Expressing yourself

I was born in 1975
rođen/rođena sam 1975
rrojen/rrojena sam teesoochoo devetsto sedamdeset petey

I came here a few years ago
došao/došla sam ovamo prije nekoliko godina
doshao/doshla sam ovdyey prreeyey nekoleeko godeena

I spent a month in Croatia last summer
proveo/provela sam mjesec dana u Hrvatskoj prošlog ljeta
prroveo/prrovela sam myesets dana oo Hrrvatskoy prroshlog lyeta

I was here last year at the same time
bio/bila sam ovdje prošle godine u isto vrijeme
beeo/beela sam ovdyey prroshley godeeney oo eesto vrreeyemey

what's the date today?
koji je danas datum?
koyee yey danas datoom?

what day is it today?
koji je danas dan?
koyee yey danas dan?

it's the 1st of May
danas je 1. svibnja
danas yey prrvee sveebnya

I'm staying until Sunday
ostajem do nedjelje
ostayem do nedyelyey

we're leaving tomorrow
sutra odlazimo
sootrra odlazeemo

I already have plans for Tuesday
već imam planove za utorak
vech eemam planovey za ootorrak

Understanding

jedanput/dvaput   once/twice
tri puta na sat/tri puta dnevno   three times an hour/a day
svakoga dana   every day
svakog ponedjeljka   every Monday

izgrađeno je polovicom devetnaestog stoljeća
it was built in the mid-nineteenth century

ovdje je ljeti velika gužva
it gets very busy here in the summer

kada odlazite?
when are you leaving?

koliko dugo ostajete?
how long are you staying?

THE TIME

Note that the 24-hour clock is often used in Croatian; 4pm may be expressed as **4 sata poslijepodne** or **16 sati**.

> **Some informal expressions**
> **u dva sata na minutu** at 2 o'clock on the dot
> **tek je prošlo osam sati** it's just gone 8 o'clock

The basics

early	rano *rrano*
half an hour	pola sata *pola sata*
in the afternoon	poslijepodne *posleeyepodney*
in the morning	ujutro *ooyootrro*
late	kasno *kasno*
midday	podne *podney*
midnight	ponoć *ponoch*
on time	na vrijeme *na vrreeyemey*
quarter of an hour	četvrt sata *chetvrrt sata*
three quarters of an hour	tričetvrtine sata *trreechetvrrteeney sata*

Expressing yourself

what time is it?
koliko je sati?
koleeko yey satee?

excuse me, have you got the time, please?
koliko je sati, molim vas?
koleeko yey satee, moleem vas?

it's exactly three o'clock
točno je tri sata (petnaest sati)
tochno yey trree sata (petnaest satee)

it's nearly one o'clock
još malo pa je jedan sat (trinaest sati)
yosh malo pa ye yedan sat (trreenaest satee)

it's ten past one
sad je jedan i deset
sad yey yedan ee deset

it's a quarter past one
sad je jedan i četvrt
sad yey yedan ee chetvrrt

it's a quarter to one
četvrt do jedan
chetvrrt do yedan

it's twenty past twelve
podne i dvadeset
podney ee dvadeset

it's twenty to twelve
jedanaest i četrdeset
yedanaest ee chetrrdeset

it's half past one
sada je trinaest i trideset
sada yey trreenaest ee trreedeset

I arrived at about two o'clock
stigao *(m)*/stigla *(f)* sam oko dva sata (četrnaest sati)
steegao/steegla sam oko dva sata (chetrrnaest satee)

I set my alarm for nine
navio *(m)*/navila *(f)* sam budilicu na devet
naveeo/naveela sam boodeeleetsoo na devet

I waited twenty minutes
čekao *(m)*/čekala *(f)* sam dvadeset minuta
chekao/chekala sam dvadeset meenoota

the train was fifteen minutes late
vlak je kasnio petnaest minuta
vlak yey kasneeo petnaest meenoota

I got home an hour ago
došao *(m)*/došla *(f)* sam kući prije sat vremena
doshao/doshla sam koochee prreeyey sat vrremena

shall we meet in half an hour?
da se nađemo za pola sata?
da sey najemo za pola sata?

I'll be back in a quarter of an hour
vratit ću se za petnaest minuta
vrateet choo sey za petnaest meenoota

there's a three-hour time difference between … and …
tri su sata vremenske razlike između … i …
tree soo sata vrremenskey razleekey eezmejoo … i …

Understanding

polasci su na puni sat i svakih pola sata
departs on the hour and the half-hour

otvoreno je od 10.00 do 16.00 sati
open from 10am to 4pm

počinje svake večeri u 19.00 sati
it's on every evening at seven

traje približno sat i pol   **otvara se u 10.00 sati**
it lasts around an hour and a half   it opens at ten in the morning

Decimal points are shown with a comma, rather than a full stop. The Croatian currency, the **kuna**, is abbreviated to **Kn** after an amount.

NUMBERS

0	nula *noola*
1	jedan *yedan*
2	dva *dva*
3	tri *trree*
4	četiri *cheteerree*
5	pet *pet*
6	šest *shest*
7	sedam *sedam*
8	osam *osam*
9	devet *devet*
10	deset *deset*
11	jedanaest *yedanaest*
12	dvanaest *dvanaest*
13	trinaest *trreenaest*
14	četrnaest *chetrrnaest*
15	petnaest *petnaest*
16	šesnaest *shesnaest*
17	sedamnaest *sedamnaest*
18	osamnaest *osamnaest*
19	devetnaest *devetnaest*
20	dvadeset *dvadeset*
21	dvadeset jedan *dvadeset yedan*
22	dvadeset dva *dvadeset dva*
30	trideset *trreedeset*
35	trideset pet *trreedeset pet*
40	četrdeset *chetrrdeset*
50	pedeset *pedeset*
60	šezdeset *shezdeset*
70	sedamdeset *sedamdeset*
80	osamdeset *osamdeset*

90	devedeset *devedeset*
100	sto *sto*
101	sto jedan *sto yedan*
200	dvjesto *dvyesto*
500	petsto *petsto*
1000	tisuću *teesoochoo*
2000	dvije tisuće *dveeyey teesoochey*
10 000	deset tisuća *deset teesoocha*
1 000 000	milijun *meeleeyoon*

first	prvi *prrvee*
second	drugi *drroogee*
third	treći *trrechee*
fourth	četvrti *chetvrrtee*
fifth	peti *petee*
sixth	šesti *shestee*
seventh	sedmi *sedmee*
eighth	osmi *osmee*
ninth	deveti *devetee*
tenth	deseti *desetee*
twentieth	dvadeseti *dvadesetee*

20 plus 3 equals 23
20 više 3 jednako 23
dvadeset veeshey trree yednako dvadeset trree

20 minus 3 equals 17
20 manje 3 jednako 17
dvadeset manyey trree yednako sedamnaest

20 multiplied by 4 equals 80
20 puta 4 jednako 80
dvadeset poota cheteerree yednako osamdeset

20 divided by 4 equals 5
20 podijeljeno sa 4 jednako 5
dvadeset podeeyelyeno sa cheteerree yednako pet

DICTIONARY

ENGLISH-CROATIAN

With most regular verbs in Croatian it is possible to form the present tense from the infinitive (see grammar). Where this is not possible the dictionary gives the first person of the present tense in brackets.

A

a (see grammar)
abbey opatija f
able: to be able to moći (mogu, možeš)
about o + loc; **to be about to do** spremati se učiniti
above iznad + gen
abroad u inozemstvu
accept prihvatiti
access pristup m **110**
accident nesreća f **30, 109**
accommodation smještaj m
across preko + gen
adaptor adapter m
address adresa f
admission pristupnina f
advance: in advance unaprijed **61**
advice savjet m; **to ask someone's advice** tražiti nečiji savjet
advise preporučiti
aeroplane zrakoplov m, avion m
after poslije
afternoon poslijepodne
after-sun (cream) krema za poslije sunčanja f
again ponovno

against protiv + gen
age dob f, godine f pl
air zrak m
air conditioning klima uređaj m
airline zrakoplovna linija f
airmail: by airmail zrakoplovom
airport zračna luka f
alarm clock budilica f
alcohol alkohol m
alive živ
all cijeli; **all day** cijeli dan; **all week** cijeli tjedan; **all the better** utoliko bolje; **all the same** svejedno; **all the time** svo vrijeme; **all inclusive** sve uračunato
allergic alergičan m, alergična f **46, 104, 106**
almost zamalo
already već
also također
although iako
always uvijek
ambulance vozilo hitne pomoći n
American (noun) Amerikanac m, Amerikanka f
American (adj) američki
among između + gen
anaesthetic anestetik m
and i

animal životinja f
ankle gležanj m
anniversary godišnjica f
another još jedan
answer *(noun)* odgovor m
answer *(v)* odgovarati
answering machine automatska
sekretarica f
ant mrav m
antibiotics antibiotici m pl
anybody, anyone svatko
anything išta
anyway u svakom slučaju
appendicitis upala f slijepog
crijeva
appointment sastanak m **103**;
to make an appointment
uročiti sastanak; **to have an**
appointment (with) imati
uročeni sastanak (s + instr)
April travanj m
area područje n; **in the area** u
okolici
arm ruka f
around oko + gen
arrange ugovoriti; **to arrange**
to meet ugovoriti susret
arrival dolazak m
arrive dolaziti
art umjetnost f
artist umjetnik m, umjetnica f
as kao; kao što; **as soon as**
possible što je prije moguće; **as**
soon as čim; netom; **as well as**
također
ashtray pepeljara f **44**
ask pitati; **to ask a question**
postaviti pitanje
aspirin aspirin m
asthma astma f **104**

at u + loc; kod + gen
attack *(v)* napadati
August kolovoz m
autumn jesen f
available dostupan m, dostupna
f
avenue avenija f
away: 10 miles away udaljen
10 milja

B

baby beba f
baby's bottle bočica f
back leđa n pl; **at the back of**
iza + gen
backpack ruksak m
bad loš; **it's not bad** nije loše
bag torba f
baggage prtljaga f
bake peći (pečem)
baker's pekara f
balcony balkon m
bandage zavoj m
bank banka f **89**
banknote novčanica f
bar bar m **61**
barbecue roštilj m
bath kada f; **to have a bath**
okupati se
bathroom kupaonica f
bath towel ručnik za kupanje m
battery akumulator m **30**
be biti *(see grammar)*
beach plaža f
beach umbrella suncobran m
beard brada f
beautiful lijep m, lijepa f
because jer; **because of** zbog
+ gen

bed krevet *m*
bee pčela *f*
before prije
begin početi (počnem)
beginner početnik *m*, početnica *f*
beginning početak *m*; **at the beginning** na početku
behind iza + *gen*
Belgian *(noun)* Belgijanac *m*, Belgijanka *f*
Belgian *(adj)* belgijski
Belgium Belgija *f*
believe vjerovati (vjerujem)
below ispod + *gen*
beside uz + *acc*; pored + *gen*
best najbolji; **the best** najbolji
better bolji; **to get better** ozdraviti; **it's better to ...** bolje je ...
between između + *gen*
bicycle bicikl *m*
bicycle pump pumpa za bicikl *f*
big velik
bike bicikl *m* **74**
bill račun *m* **48**, **49**
bin kanta za smeće *f*
binoculars dvogled *m*
birthday rođendan *m*
bit komadić *m*
bite *(noun)* ugriz *m*
bite *(v)* gristi (grizem) **103**
black crn
blackout gubitak svijesti *m*
blanket pokrivač *m*
bleed krvariti
bless: bless you! nazdravlje!
blind *(adj)* slijep
blister plik *m*
blood krv *f*
blood pressure krvni tlak *m*

blue plav
board *(v)* ukrcati **25**
boarding ukrcaj *m*
boat brod *m*
body tijelo *n*
book *(noun)* knjiga *f*; **book of tickets** blok karata *m*
book *(v)* rezervirati **23**, **61**
bookshop knjižara *f*
boot *(of car)* prtljažnik *m*
borrow posuditi
botanical garden botanički vrt *m*
both oboje; **both of us** i jedan i drugi
bottle boca *f*
bottle opener otvarač za boce *m*
bottom dno *n*, podnožje; **at the bottom** na dnu; **at the bottom of** u podnožju
bowl zdjela *f*
bra grudnjak *m*
brake *(noun)* kočnica *f*
brake *(v)* kočiti
bread kruh *m* **47**
break slomiti; **to break one's leg** slomiti nogu
break down pokvariti **30**, **110**
breakdown kvar na automobilu *m*
breakdown service služba za pomoć na cesti (HAK) *f*
breakfast doručak *m* **37**; **to have breakfast** doručkovati (doručkujem)
bridge most *m*
bring donositi
brochure brošura *f*
broken slomljen
bronchitis bronhitis *m*

brother brat *m*
brown smeđ
brush četka *f*
build graditi
building zgrada *f*
bump čvoruga *f; (on road)* ispupčenje *n*
bumper branik *m*
buoy bova *f*
burn *(noun)* opeklina *f*
burn *(v)* opeći (opečem)
burst *(v)* rasprsnuti se (rasprsnem se)
burst *(adj)* rasprsnut
bus autobus *m* **28**
bus route autobusna linija *f*
bus station autobusni kolodvor *m*
bus stop autobusna postaja *f*
busy *(person)* zaposlen; *(street)* prometan *m*, prometna *f*
but ali
butcher's mesnica *f*
buy kupovati (kupujem) **78**, **80**
by kod + *gen;* **by car** automobilom
bye! zbogom!, doviđenja!; *(informal)* papa!

C

café kafić *m*
call *(noun)* poziv *m*
call *(v)* zvati (zovem) **98**
call back uzvratiti poziv **98**
camera fotoaparat *m*
camper kampist *m*
camping kampiranje *n;* **to go camping** ići kampirati
camping stove kuhalo za kampiranje *n*

campsite kamp *m* **41**
can *(noun)* konzerva *n*
can *(v)* moći; **I can't** ne mogu
cancel otkazivati (otkazujem)
candle svijeća *f*
can opener otvarač za konzerve *m*
car automobil *m*
caravan stambena prikolica *f*
card ulaznica *f*
car park parkiralište *n*
carry nositi
case: in case of ... u slučaju ... + *gen*
cash gotovina *f;* **to pay in cash** plaćati gotovinom **80**
cashpoint bankomat *m* **89**
castle dvorac *m*
catch uhvatiti
cathedral katedrala *f*
CD CD *m*
cemetery groblje *n*
centimetre centimetar *m*
centre centar *m* **37**
century stoljeće *n*
chair stolica *f*
chairlift sedežnica *f*
change *(noun)* zamjena *f; (money)* sitan novac *m* **79**,**80**
change *(v)* razmijeniti **89**
changing room kabina za presvlačenje *f* **82**
channel valna dužina *f*
chapel kapelica *f*
charge *(noun)* pristojba *f*
charge *(v)* naplaćivati (naplaćujem)
cheap jeftin
check kontrola *f*
check-in registracija putnika *f* **25**

check in *(to hotel)* prijaviti boravak u hotelu; *(at airport)* registrirati putnike
checkout blagajna *f*
cheers! živjeli!
chemist's ljekarna *f*
cheque ček *m*
chest prsa *f*
child dijete *n*
chilly hladan *m*, hladna *f*
chimney dimnjak *m*
chin brada *f*
church crkva *f*
cigar cigara *f*
cigarette cigareta *f*
cigarette papers rizle *f pl*
cinema kinematograf *m*, kino *n*
circus cirkus *m*
city velegrad *m*
clean *(adj)* čist
clean *(v)* čistiti
cliff litica *f*
climate klima *f*
climbing penjanje *n*
cloakroom garderoba *f*
close *(v)* zatvoriti
closed zatvoren
closing time vrijeme zatvaranja *n*
clothes odjeća *f*
clutch *(noun)* kvačilo *n*
coach autobus *m*
coast obala *f*
coathanger vješalica za kapute *f*
cockroach žohar *m*
coffee kava *f* **48**
coil *(contraceptive)* spirala *f*
coin novčić *f*
Coke® Coca Cola *f* **47**
cold *(noun)* hladnoća *f*; **to have a cold** biti prehlađen

cold *(adj)* studen; **it's cold** studeno je; **I'm cold** studeno mi je
collection kolekcija *f*
colour boja *f* **82**
comb češalj *m*
come dolaziti
come back vratiti se
come in ulaziti
come out izlaziti
comfortable udoban *m*, udobna *f*
company kompanija *f*
compartment odjeljak *m*
complain žaliti se
comprehensive insurance kasko osiguranje *n* **31**
computer kompjuter *m*
concert koncert *m* **61**
concert hall koncertna dvorana *f*
concession povlastica *f* **23**, **67**
condom prezervativ *m*
confirm potvrđivati (potvrđujem) **25**
connection veza *f* **26**
constipated: to be constipated imati zatvor
consulate poslanstvo *n* **109**
contact *(noun)* doticaj *m*
contact *(v)* stupiti u vezu, kontaktirati **97**
contact lenses kontaktne leće *f pl*
contagious zarazan *m*, zarazna *f*
contraceptive sredstvo za kontracepciju *n*
cook kuhati
cooked kuhan
cooking kuhati; **to do the cooking** skuhati

cool svjež; **this is cool** to je štosno

corkscrew vadičep *m*

correct točan *m*, točna *f*

cost (noun) cijena *f*

cost (v) stajati; **how much does it cost?** koliko stoji?

cotton pamuk *m*

cotton bud štapići za uši *m*

cotton wool vata *f*

cough (noun) kašalj *m*; **to have a cough** imati kašalj

cough (v) kašljati (kašljem)

count brojati (brojim)

country zemlja *f*

countryside selo *n*, priroda *f*

course: of course dakako

cover (noun) pokrivač *m*

cover (v) pokrivati

credit card kreditna kartica *f* **35, 49, 80, 89**

cross (noun) križ *m*

cross (v) prelaziti

cruise kružno putovanje *n*

cry plakati (plačem)

cup šalica *f*

currency valuta *f*

customs carinarnica *f*

cut (v) rezati (režem); **to cut oneself** porezati se

cycle path biciklistička staza *f* **74**

D

damaged oštećen

damp vlaga *f*

dance (noun) ples *m*

dance (v) plesati (plešem)

dangerous opasan *m*, opasna *f*

dark taman *m*, tamna *f*; **dark blue** tamnoplav

date (noun) datum *m*; **out of date** zastario *m*, zastarjela *f*

date (v) **to date from** datirati od

date of birth datum rođenja *m*

daughter kćer *f*

day dan *m*; **the day after tomorrow** prekosutra; **the day before yesterday** prekjučer

dead mrtav *m*, mrtva *f*

deaf gluh

dear drag

debit card kartica tekućeg računa *f*

December prosinac *m*

declare prijaviti

deep dubok

degree stupanj *m*

delay zastoj *m*

delayed: the plane is delayed avion kasni

delight radost *f*

dentist zubar *m*

deodorant dezodorans *m*

department odjel *m*

department store robna kuća *f*

departure polazak *m*

depend: that depends (on) to ovisi (o + *loc*)

deposit polog *m*

dessert desert *m* **46**

develop: to get a film developed razviti film **86**

diabetes šećerna bolest *f*

dialling code pozivni broj *m*

diarrhoea: to have diarrhoea imati proljev

die umrijeti

diesel dizel *m*

diet dijeta *f*; **to be on a diet** biti na dijeti
different različit
difficult težak *m*, teška *f*
digital camera digitalna kamera *f*
dinner večera *f*; **to have dinner** večerati
direct izravan *m*, izravna *f*
direction smjer *m*; **to have a good sense of direction** dobro se orijentirati
directory imenik *m*
directory enquiries služba informacija *f*
dirty *(adj)* prljav
disabled invalidna osoba *f* **110**
disaster velika nesreća *f*, katastrofa *f*
disco disko *m*
discount popust *m* **66**; **to give someone a discount** dati nekome popust
discount fare povlastica na vožnju *f*
dish jelo *n*; **dish of the day** jelo dana *n*
dishes suđe *n*; **to do the dishes** prati suđe
dish towel krpa za suđe *f*
dishwasher perilica za suđe *f*
disinfect dezinficirati
disposable za jednokratnu uporabu
disturb uznemiravati; **do not disturb** ne ometaj
dive roniti
diving: to go diving ići na ronjenje
do činiti; **do you have a light?** imate li vatre?

doctor liječnik *m*, liječnica *f* **102**
door vrata *n pl*
door code zaporka za vrata *f*
downstairs dolje
draught beer točeno pivo *n*
dress: to get dressed odjenuti se
dressing zavoj *m*
drink *(noun)* piće *n*; **to go for a drink** ići na piće **44**, **58**; **to have a drink** popiti piće
drink *(v)* piti (pijem)
drinking water pitka voda *f*
drive *(noun)* **to go for a drive** ići na vožnju
drive *(v)* voziti
driving licence vozačka dozvola *f*
drops kapi *m pl*
drown utopiti se
drugs lijekovi *m pl*
drunk pijan
dry *(adj)* suh
dry *(v)* sušiti
dry cleaner's kemijska čistionica *f*
duck raca *f*, patka *f*
during tijekom + *gen*; **during the week** tijekom tjedna
dustbin kanta za smeće *f*
duty chemist's dežurna ljekarna *f*

each svaki; **each one** svaki pojedini
ear uho *n* (*pl* uši *f*)
early rani
earplugs čepići za uši *m pl*

earrings naušnice f pl
earth zemlja f
east istok m; **in the east** na istoku; **(to the) east of** istočno od
Easter Uskrs m
easy lagan
eat jesti (jedem) **44**
economy class turistička klasa f
Elastoplast® flaster m
electric električni
electricity struja f
electricity meter mjerilo za struju n
electric shaver električni brijač m
e-mail e-mail m **94**
e-mail address e-mail adresa f **18, 94**
embassy veleposlanstvo n
emergency hitan slučaj m **109**; **in an emergency** u slučaju nužde f
emergency exit izlaz u slučaju nužde m
empty prazan m, prazna f
end kraj m; **at the end of** na kraju; **at the end of the street** na kraju ulice
engaged zauzet **99**
engine stroj m
England Engleska f
English engleski
enjoy: enjoy your meal! u-slast!; **to enjoy oneself** uživati
enough dosta; **that's enough** sad je dosta
entrance ulaz m
envelope kuverta f

epileptic epileptičar m
equipment oprema f
espresso espresso m
Europe Europa f
European *(noun)* Europljanin m, Europljanka f
European *(adj)* europski
evening večer f; **in the evening** uvečer; tijekom večeri
every svaki; **every day** svakodnevno
everybody, everyone svatko
everywhere posvuda
except izuzev
exceptional izuzetan m, izuzetna f
excess prekoračenje n; **excess baggage** prekoračenje dozvoljene težine n
exchange mijenjati
exchange rate devizni tečaj m
excuse *(noun)* isprika f
excuse *(v)* **excuse me** oprostite
exhausted iscrpljen
exhaust pipe ispušna cijev f
exhibition izložba f **66**
exit izlaz m
expensive skup
expiry date rok isteka valjanosti m
express *(adj)* žurni
expresso espresso m
extra dodatan m, dodatna f
eye oko n *(pl* oči f*)*

F

face lice n
facecloth krpica za pranje lica f
fact činjenica f; **in fact** ustvari

faint (v) onesvijestiti se
fair (noun) sajam m
fall (v) padati; **to fall asleep** zaspati; **to fall ill** razboliti se
family obitelj f
fan ventilator m
far dalek; **far from** daleko od
fare cijena vožnje f
fast brz
fast-food restaurant fast food restoran m
fat mastan m, masna f
father otac m
favour usluga f; **to do someone a favour** učiniti nekome uslugu
favourite omiljen
fax faks m
February veljača f
fed up: to be fed up (with) biti sit (+ gen)
feel osjećati se 103; **to feel good/bad** osjećati se dobro/loše
feeling osjećaj m
ferry trajekt m
festival festival m
fetch: to go and fetch someone/something dovesti dovedem/donijeti donesem
fever povišena temperatura f; **to have a fever** imati povišenu temperaturu
few nekoliko
fiancé zaručnik m
fiancée zaručnica f
fight (noun) sukob m
fill ulijevati (ulijevam)
fill in (form) ispuniti
fill out (form) ispuniti
fill up: to fill up with petrol napuniti rezervoar benzinom
filling (in tooth) plomba f
film (for camera) film m 86
finally konačno
find naći (nađem) 18
fine (noun) globa f
fine (adj) dobar m, dobra f
finger prst m
finish završiti
fire vatra f; **fire!** gori vatra!
fire brigade vatrogasci m pl
fireworks vatromet m
first prvi; **first (of all)** kao prvo
first class prvi razred m
first floor prvi kat m
first name ime n
fish (noun) riba f
fishmonger's ribarnica f
fish shop ribarnica f
fitting room kabina za presvlačenje f
fizzy gaziran
flash bljeskalica f 86
flask termos boca f
flat (adj) spljošten; **flat tyre** prazna guma f
flat (noun) stan m
flavour aroma f
flaw (in garment) poderotina f
flight let m
flip-flops japanke f pl
floor (storey) kat m; **on the floor** na podu
flu gripa f
fly (noun) muha f
fly (v) letjeti (letim)
food hrana f 80
food poisoning trovanje hranom n
foot stopalo n

for za + *acc*; **for an hour** za sat
forbidden zabranjen
forecast prognoza *f*
forehead čelo *n*
foreign inozeman *m*, inozemna *f*
foreigner stranac *m*, strankinja *f*
forest šuma *f*
fork viljuška *f*
former bivši
forward *(adj)* prednji
four-star petrol euro super 95 *m*
fracture lom *m*
fragile lomljiv
France Francuska *f*
free slobodan *m*, slobodna *f*;
(without charge) besplatan *m*,
besplatna *f* **65**
freezer zamrzivač *m*
French francuski
Friday petak *m*
fridge hladnjak *m*
fried pržen
friend prijatelj *m*, prijateljica *f*
from od + *gen*; **from … to …**
od … do …
front prednji dio *m*; **in front of**
ispred
fry pržiti
frying pan tava *f*
full pun; **full of** do vrha pun + *gen*
full board pansion *m*
full fare, full price puna cijena
(vožnje) *f* **67**
funfair zabavište *n*
fuse osigurač *m*

G

gallery galerija *f*
game igra *f* **76**

garage garaža *f*; *(for repairs)*
automehaničarska radionica *f* **30**
garden vrt *m*
gas plin *m*
gas cylinder plinska svjetiljka *f*
gastric flu crijevna gripa *f*
gate izlaz *m*
gauze gaza *f*
gay homoseksualan
gearbox mjenjač *m*
general opći
gents' (toilet) muški WC *m*
German *(noun)* Nijemac *m*,
Njemica *f*
German *(adj)* njemački
Germany Njemačka *f*
get dobivati
get off *(boat)* iskrcati se; *(bus,*
train) silaziti **28**
get up ustajati (ustajem)
gift wrap papir za zamotavanje
poklona *m*
girl djevojka *f*
girlfriend djevojka *f*; *(informal)*
cura *f*
give davati (dajem)
give back vraćati
glass čaša *f*; **a glass of water/**
wine čaša vode/vina
glasses naočale *f pl*
gluten-free ne sadrži gluten
go ići (idem) **58**; **to go to**
Zagreb/to Croatia ići u
Zagreb/ići u Hrvatsku; **we're**
going home tomorrow sutra
idemo kući
go away odlaziti
go in ulaziti
go out izlaziti
go with ići s + *instr*

golf golf *m*
golf course teren za golf *m*
good dobar *m*, dobra *f*; **good morning** dobro jutro; **good afternoon** dobar dan; **good evening** dobra večer
goodbye doviđenja
goodnight laku noć
goods dobra *n pl*
GP liječnik opće prakse *m*
grams grami *m pl* **81**
grass trava *f*
great velik
Great Britain Velika Britanija *f*
Greece Grčka *f*
Greek *(noun)* Grk *m*, Grkinja *f*
Greek *(adj)* grčki
green zelen
grey siv
grocer's trgovina mješovite robe *f*
ground osnova *f*; **on the ground** na temelju
ground floor prizemlje *n*
ground sheet štep-deka *f*
grow rasti (rastem)
guarantee garancija *f*
guest gost *m*
guest house gostionica *f*
guide vodič *m* **60**
guidebook vodič *m*
guided tour turistički obilazak u pratnji vodiča *m*
gynaecologist ginekolog *m*, ginekologinja *f*

H

hair kosa *f*
hairdresser frizer *m*, frizerka *f*

hairdrier sušilo za kosu *n*
half pola; **half a litre/kilo** pola litre/pola kilograma; **half an hour** pola sata
half-board polupansion *m*
half-pint: a half-pint pola pinte
hand ruka *f*
handbag ručna torbica *f*
handbrake ručna kočnica *f*
handicapped hendikepiran
handkerchief rupčić *m*
hand luggage ručna prtljaga *f* **25**
hand-made ručni rad
hangover mamurluk *m*
happen dogoditi se
happy sretan *m*, sretna *f*
hard tvrd
hashish hašiš *m*
hat šešir *m*
hate mrziti
have imati
have to morati; **I have to go** moram poći
hay fever peludna groznica *f*
he on *(see grammar)*
head glava *f*
headache: to have a headache imati glavobolju
headlight far *m*
health zdravlje *n*
hear čuti (čujem)
heart srce *n*
heart attack srčani udar *m*
heat vrućina *f*
heating grijanje *n*
heavy težak *m*, teška *f*
hello halo
helmet kaciga *f*
help *(noun)* pomoć *f*; **to call**

for help pozvati pomoć; **help!** upomoć!

help *(v)* pomagati (pomažem) **109**

her *(see grammar)*

here ovdje; **here is/are** evo + *gen*

hers njezin

hi! bok!

hi-fi hi-fi *m*

high visok

high blood pressure visoki krvni tlak *m*

high tide plima *f*

hiking rekreativno pješačenje *n* **72**; **to go hiking** ići na rekreativno pješačenje

hill brdo *n*

hill-walking planinarenje *n*; **to go hill-walking** planinariti

him *(see grammar)*

hip kuk *m*

hire *(noun)* najam *m*

hire *(v) (pay for hire of)* unajmiti **31**, **71**, **73**, **74**; *(hire out)* iznajmiti

his njegov

hitchhike autostopirati

hitchhiking autostopiranje

hold držati (držim)

hold on! *(on the phone)* pričekajte trenutak!

holiday(s) odmor *m*; **on holiday** na odmoru **16**

holiday camp ljetovalište *n*

Holland Holandija *f*

home dom *m*; kuća *f*; **at home** doma; **to go home** ići kući

homosexual homoseksualan

honest pošten

honeymoon medeni mjesec *m*

horse konj *m*

hospital bolnica *f*

hot vruć; **it's hot** vruće je; **hot drink** toplo piće *n*

hot chocolate vruća čokolada *f*

hotel hotel *m*

hotplate plak *n*

hour sat *m*; **an hour and a half** sat i pol

house kuća *f*

housework kućni poslovi *m pl*; **to do the housework** pospremati kuću

how kako; **how are you?** kako ste?

hunger glad *f*

hungry: to be hungry biti gladan *m*, gladna *f*

hurry *(noun)* **to be in a hurry** žuriti se

hurry (up) požuri!

hurt: it hurts boli me; **my head hurts** boli me glava **103**, **104**

husband suprug *m*

I

I ja; **I'm English** ja sam Englez/ Engleskinja; **I'm 22 (years old)** 22 su mi godine

ice led

ice cube kocka leda *f*

identity card osobna iskaznica *f*

identity papers dokumenti *m pl*

if ako

ill bolestan *m*, bolesna *f*

illness bolest *f*

important važan *m*, važna *f*

in u, na; **in 2006** u 2006.god.;

in Croatia u Hrvatskoj; **in the 19th century** u 19. stoljeću; **in an hour** za sat
included uračunat **37**, **40**, **49**
independent nezavisan *m*, nezavisna *f*
indicator brojilo *n*
infection infekcija *f*
information obavijest *f* **65**
injection injekcija *f*
injured ozlijeđen
insect insekt *m*
insecticide insekticid *m*
inside unutra
insomnia nesanica *f*
instant coffee instant kava *f*
instead umjesto; **instead of** umjesto + *gen*
insurance osiguranje *n*
intend to namjeravati
international međunarodni
international money order međunarodni platni nalog
Internet Internet *m*
Internet café Internet cafe *m* **93**
invite pozivati
Ireland Irska
Irish irski
iron *(noun)* glačalo *n*
iron *(v)* glačati
island otok
it ono/to; **it's beautiful** lijepo je; **it's warm** toplo je
Italian *(noun)* Talijan *(m)*, Talijanka *(f)*
Italian *(adj)* talijanski
Italy Italija
itchy: it's itchy svrbi me
item predmet *m*, stvar *f*

J

jacket jakna *f*
January siječanj *m*
jetlag jetlag *m*
jeweller's zlatarnica *f*
jewellery nakit *m*
job posao *m*
jogging jogging *m*
journey putovanje *n*
jug vrč *m*
juice sok *m*
July srpanj *m*
jumper džemper *m*
June lipanj *m*
just: just before malo prije; **just a little** samo malo; **just one** samo jedan; **I've just arrived** upravo sam stigao/stigla; **just in case** za svaki slučaj

K

kayak kajak *m*
keep čuvati
key ključ *m* **37**, **39**
kidney bubreg *m*
kill ubiti (ubijem)
kilometre kilometar *m*
kind: what kind of …? koje vrste ...?
kitchen kuhinja *f*
knee koljeno *n*
knife nož *m*
knock down srušiti
know znati; **I don't know** ne znam

L

ladies' (toilet) ženski WC *m*

lake jezero n
lamp svjetiljka f
landmark znamenitost f
landscape krajolik m
language jezik m
laptop laptop m
last *(adj)* prošli; **last year** prošle
godine
last *(v)* trajati (trajem)
late kasni **26**
laugh smijati se (smijem se)
launderette praonica rublja f
lawyer odvjetnik m odvjetnica f
leaflet letak m
leak curiti
learn učiti
least: the least najmanje; **at
least** barem
leave ostaviti
left lijevi; **to the left (of)** lijevo
od
left-luggage (office) garderoba f
leg noga f
lend posuditi
lens leća f
lenses leće f pl
less manje; **less than** manje
nego
let dozvoliti
letter pismo n
letterbox sandučić za poštu m
library knjižnica f
life život m
lift dizalo n **37**
light *(adj)* svijetli; **light blue**
svijetloplava
light *(noun)* vatra; **do you have a
light?** imate li vatre?
light *(v)* pripaliti
light bulb žarulja f

lighter upaljač m
lighthouse svjetionik
like *(adv)* jednako, slično
like *(v)* voljeti (volim) **18**; **I'd like
... želim ... 8**
line crta f; *(queue)* red m
lip usnica f
listen slušati
listings magazine oglasnik m
litre litra f
little *(adj)* malen
little *(adv)* malo
live živjeti (živim)
liver jetra f
living room dnevna soba f
local time lokalno vrijeme n
lock *(noun)* brava f
lock *(v)* zabraviti
long dug; **a long time** dugo
vremena; **how long ... ?** koliko
dugo ...?
look izgled; **to look tired**
izgledati umorno
look after brinuti o nekome
look at gledati
look for tražiti **78**
look like nalikovati; izgledati
what does he look like? kako
on izgleda?
lorry kamion m
lose izgubiti **110**; **to get lost**
izgubiti se; **to be lost** biti
izgubljen **12**
lot: a lot (of) mnogo
loud glasan m, glasna f
low nizak m, niska f
low blood pressure niski krvni
tlak m
low-fat niskokaloričan
low tide oseka f

luck sreća f
lucky: to be lucky biti sretan, sretna
luggage prtljaga f **26**
lukewarm mlak
lunch objed; **to have lunch** objedovati
lungs pluća n pl
luxury *(noun)* luksuz m
luxury *(adj)* luksuzan m, luksuzna f

M

magazine časopis m
maiden name djevojačko prezime n
mail poštanske pošiljke f pl
main glavni
main course glavno jelo n
make činiti
man muškarac m, čovjek m
manage uspijevati
manager menadžer m
many puno; **how many?** koliko?; **how many times …?** koliko puta …?
map zemljovid m, plan grada m **12**, **59**, **65**
March ožujak m
marina marina f
market tržnica f **81**
married vjenčani
mass misa f
match *(for fire)* šibica f; *(game)* utakmica f
material materijal n
matter: it doesn't matter nije bitno
mattress madrac m
May svibanj m

maybe možda
me *(see grammar)*; **me too** i ja
meal obrok n
mean značiti; **what does … mean?** što znači …?
medicine lijek n
medium srednji; *(meat)* srednje pečeno/kuhano
meet susresti, naći se s nekim **59**
meeting sastanak m
member član m
menu jelovnik m
message poruka f **97**
meter mjerilo n
metre metar m
microwave mikrovalna pećnica f
midday podne n
middle sredina f; **in the middle (of)** u sredini (+ gen)
midnight ponoć f
might: it might rain možda će kišiti
mill mlin m
mind: I don't mind ne smeta me
mine moj
mineral water mineralna voda f
minute minuta f; **at the last minute** u posljednjem trenutku
mirror zrcalo n
Miss gospođica f
miss propustiti **26**, **28**; nedostajati; **we missed the train** propustili smo vlak; **there are two … missing** nedostaju dva …
mistake pogreška; **to make a mistake** pogriješiti
mobile (phone) mobitel m **97**

modern suvremen

moisturizer krema za lice *f*

moment trenutak *m*; **at the moment** u ovom trenutku

monastery manastir *m*

Monday ponedjeljak *m*

money novac *m* 79

month mjesec *m*

monument spomenik *m*

mood: to be in a good/bad mood biti dobre/zle volje

moon mjesec *m*

moped moped *m*

more više; **more than** više nego; **much more, a lot more** puno više, znatno više; **there's no more ...** nema više ...

morning jutro *n*

morning-after pill pilula za dan poslije *f* 106

mosque džamija *f*

mosquito komarac *m*

most: the most većina; **most people** većina ljudi

mother majka *f*

motorbike motorkotač *m*

motorway autocesta *f*

mountain planina *f*

mountain bike brdski bicikl *m*

mountain hut planinarska koliba *f*

mouse miš *m*

mouth usta *n pl*

movie film *m*

Mr gospodin *m*

Mrs gospođa *f*

much: how much? mnogo; **how much is it?, how much does it cost?** koliko je to?, koliko to stoji?

muscle mišić *m*

museum muzej *m*

music glazba *f*

must morati; **it must be 5 o'clock** mora biti 17.00 sati; **I must go** moram ići

my moj

nail nokat *m*

naked gol

name ime *n*; **my name is ...** ime mi je ... 14

nap drijemati; **to have a nap** malo zadrijemati

napkin ubrus *m*

nappy pelena *f*

national holiday državni blagdan *m*

nature priroda *f*

near blizu + *gen*; **near the beach** pored plaže; **the nearest ...** najbliži ...

necessary neophodan *m*, neophodna *f*

neck vrat *m*

need trebati

neighbour susjed *m*, susjeda *f*

neither: neither do I ni ja; **neither ... nor ...** ni ... niti ...

nervous živčan

Netherlands Nizozemska *f*

never nikada

new nov

news *(item)* vijest *f*; *(on radio, TV)* vijesti *f pl*

newsagent prodavač novina *m*

newspaper novine *f pl*

newsstand novinarnica *f*, kiosk *m*

New Year Nova godina f
next slijedeći
nice zgodan m, zgodna f
night noć f **137**
nightclub noćni klub m
nightdress spavaćica f
no ne; **no, thank you** ne, hvala; **no idea** nemam ideju
nobody nitko
noise buka f; **to make a noise** bučiti
noisy bučan m, bučna f
non-drinking water voda koja nije za piće f
none nijedan, nijedna
non-smoker nepušač m
noon podne n
no one nitko
north sjever m; **in the north** na sjeveru; **(to the) north of** sjeverno od
nose nos m
not ne; **not yet** još ne; **not any** nijedan; **not at all** nipošto
note novčanica f
notebook notes m
nothing ništa
novel roman m
November studeni m
now sada
nowadays dan danas
nowhere nigdje
number broj m
nurse medicinska sestra f

O

obvious očigledan m, očigledna f
ocean ocean m
o'clock: one o'clock sat m;

three o'clock tri sata
October listopad m
of od + gen, iz + gen
offer (noun) ponuda f
often često
oil ulje n
ointment mast f
OK OK, dobro
old star; **how old are you?** koliko vam je godina?; **old people** stariji ljudi
old town stari grad m
on na; **it's on at ...** počinje u ...
once jedanput; **once a day/an hour** jedanput dnevno/svaki sat
one jedan
only sam
open (adj) otvoren **67**
open (v) otvoriti
operate upravljati
operation: to have an operation ići na operaciju
opinion mišljenje n; **in my opinion** po mome mišljenju
opportunity prilika f
opposite (noun) suprotnost f
opposite (prep) preko puta + gen
optician optičar m, optičarka f
or ili
orange naranča f
orchestra orkestar m
order (noun) red m; (of food) narudžba f; **out of order** u kvaru
order (v) naručiti **46**, **79**
organic organski
organize organizirati
other drugi; **others** ostali
otherwise na drugi način; inače
our naš
ours naš

outside vani
outward journey odlazak *m*
oven pećnica *f*
over: over there tamo prijeko
overdone prekuhan; prepečen
overweight: my luggage is overweight moja prtljaga je iznad dopuštene težine
owe dugovati (dugujem) 48, 79
own *(adj)* vlastiti; **my own car** moj vlastiti automobil
own *(v)* posjedovati (posjedujem)
owner vlasnik *m*, vlasnica *f*

P

pack: to pack one's suitcase pakirati svoj kovčeg/kofer
package holiday paket aranžman *m*
packed pretrpan
packet poštanska pošiljka *f*
painting slika *f*
pair par *m*; **a pair of pyjamas** pidžama *f*; **a pair of shorts** kratke hlačice *f pl*
palace dvorac *m*
pants hlače *f pl*
paper papir *m*; **paper napkin** papirnati ubrus *m*; **paper tissue** papirnati rupčić *f*
parcel poštanska pošiljka *f*
pardon? oprostite?
parents roditelji *m pl*
park *(noun)* park *m*
park *(v)* parkirati
parking space parkiralište *n*
part dio *m*; **to be a part of ...** biti dijelom ...
party zabava *f*

pass *(noun)* propusnica *f*
pass *(v)* prolaziti
passenger putnik *m*
passport putovnica *f*
past poslije + *gen*; **a quarter past ten** deset sati i petnaest minuta
path staza *f* 73
patient pacijent *m*
pay platiti 79, 80
pedestrian pješak *m*
pedestrianized street pješačka zona *f*
pee piškiti
peel guliti
pen pero *n*
pencil olovka *f*
people ljudi *m pl*, narod *m* 45
percent postotak *m*
perfect perfektan
perfume parfem *m*
perhaps možda
period mjesečnica *f*
person osoba *f*
personal stereo osobni stereo *m*
petrol gorivo *n* 30
petrol station benzinska crpka *f*
phone *(noun)* telefon *m*
phone *(v)* telefonirati, nazvati
phone box telefonska govornica *f* 97
phone call telefonski poziv *m*; **to make a phone call** nazvati nekoga
phonecard telefonska kartica *f* 96
phone number telefonski broj *m*
photo fotografija *f*; **to take a**

photo (of) fotografirati **85**; **to take someone's photo** fotografirati nekoga

picnic piknik m; **to have a picnic** piknikovati

pie pita f

piece komad m; **a piece of** komad + gen; **a piece of fruit** komad voća

piles hemeroidi m pl

pill pilula f; **to be on the pill** uzimati pilulu **104**

pillow jastuk m

pillowcase jastučnica f

PIN (number) PIN m

pink ružičast

pity: it's a pity šteta je

place mjesto n

plan plan m **58**

plane zrakoplov m, avion m

plant biljka f

plaster (cast) gips m

plastic plastika f

plastic bag plastična vrećica f **79**

plate tanjur m

platform peron m **28**

play (n) kazališna predstava f

play (v) igrati se

please molim

pleased zadovoljan m, zadovoljna f; **pleased to meet you!** drago mi je!

pleasure zadovoljstvo n

plug utikač m

plug in uključiti

plumber vodoinstalater m

point točka f

police policija f

policeman policajac m

police station policijska postaja f **109**

policewoman policajka f

poor siromašan m, siromašna f

port luka f

portrait portret m

Portugal Portugal m

Portuguese (n) Portugalac m, Portugalka f

Portuguese (adj) portugalski

possible moguć

post pošta f **92**

postbox poštanski sandučić m **92**

postcard poštanska dopisnica f; (with picture) razglednica f

postcode poštanski broj m

poster poster m

poste restante poste restante

postman poštar m

post office poštanski ured m, pošta f **92**

pot lonac m

pound funta f

practical praktičan m, praktična f

pram dječja kolica f

prefer više voljeti (volim)

pregnant trudna **104**

prepare prirediti

present dar m **83**

press pritisnuti (pritisnem)

pressure tlak m

previous prethodan m, prethodna f

price cijena f

private privatan m, privatna f

prize nagrada f

probably najvjerojatnije

problem problem m

procession procesija *f*
product proizvod *m*
profession zanimanje *n*, profesija *f*
programme program *m*; *(on radio, TV)* emisija *f*
promise obećati
propose predlagati (predlažem)
protect zaštititi
proud (of) biti ponosan *m*, ponosna *f* (na + *acc*)
public javnost *f*, publika *f*
public holiday javni blagdan *m*
pull vući (vučem)
purple ljubičast
purpose: on purpose namjerno
purse novčanik *m*
push gurnuti
pushchair kolica *f*
put metnuti (metnem)
put out iznijeti (iznesem)
put up with podnositi

quality kakvoća *f*; **of good/bad quality** dobre/loše kakvoće
quarter četvrtina *f*; **a quarter of an hour** četvrt sata; **a quarter to ten** četvrt do deset
quay pristanište *n*, molo *n*
question pitanje *n*
queue *(noun)* rep *m*
queue *(v)* čekati u repu
quick brz
quickly brzo
quiet miran *m*, mirna *f*
quite posve; **quite a lot of** puno

racist rasist *m*, rasistica *f*
racket reket *m*
radiator radijator *m*
radio radio *m*
radio station radio postaja *f*
rain *(noun)* kiša *f*
rain *(v)* **it's raining** kiši
raincoat kišni ogrtač *m*
random: at random nasumce
rape silovanje *n*
rare rijedak *m*, rijetka *f*
rarely rijetko
rather prilično; **I'd rather ...** radije bih ...
raw sirov
razor brijač *m*
razor blade žilet *m*
reach dosegnuti, doći do
read čitati
ready spreman *m*, spremna *f*
reasonable razborit
receipt potvrda o primitku *f* 80, 105
receive primati
reception recepcija *f*; **at reception** na recepciji 39
receptionist recepcionist *m*, recepcionistica *f*
recipe recept *m*
recognize prepoznati
recommend preporučiti 37, 44
red crven; *(hair)* riđokos
red light crveno svjetlo *n*
red wine crno vino *n*
reduce smanjiti
reduction popust *m*, sniženje *n*
refrigerator hladnjak *m*
refund *(noun)* naknada *f*; **to get**

a refund dobiti naknadu **83**
refund (v) nadoknaditi **105**
refuse odbiti
registered registriran
registration number registarske pločice f pl
remember sjećati se
remind podsjetiti
remove ukloniti
rent (noun) stanarina f
rent (v) (pay for hire of) unajmiti **39**; (hire out) iznajmiti
rental najam m
reopen ponovno otvoriti
repair (v) popravljati **30**; **to get something repaired** dati nešto popraviti
repeat ponoviti **10**
reserve rezervirati **45**
reserved rezerviran
rest (noun) **the rest** ostatak m
rest (v) odmarati se
restaurant restoran m **44**
return povratak m
return ticket povratna karta f
reverse-charge call poziv na račun nazvanog m **96**
reverse gear rikverc n
rheumatism reumatizam m
rib rebro n
right (n) pravo n; **to have the right to …** imati pravo učiniti …; **to the right (of)** desno od
right (adj) (correct) točan m, točna f; (not left) desni
right (adv) **right away** odmah; **right beside** točno pored
ring zvono n
ripe zreo m, zrela f
rip-off pljačka f

risk rizik m
river rijeka f
road cesta f
road sign prometni znak m
rock stijena f
rollerblades koturaljke f pl
room soba f **36**, **37**
rosé wine ružica f
round okrugao m, okrugla f
roundabout kružni tok m
rubbish smeće n; **to take the rubbish out** iznijeti smeće
rucksack ruksak m
rug tepih m
ruins ruševina f; **in ruins** u ruševinama
run out: to have run out of petrol ostati bez benzina

S

sad tužan m, tužna f
safe bezopasan m, bezopasna f
safety sigurnost f
safety belt sigurnosni pojas m
sail jedro n
sailing jedrenje n; **to go sailing** jedriti
sale: for sale na prodaju; **in the sale** na rasprodaji
sales rasprodaje f pl
salt sol f
salted usoljen
salty slan
same isti; **the same** isti **48**
sand pijesak m
sandals sandale f pl
sanitary towel uložak m, higijenski uložak m
Saturday subota f

saucepan lonac m
save sačuvati
say kazati (kažem); **how do you say … ?** kako kažete …?
scared: to be scared (of) uplašiti se (+ gen)
scenery krajobraz m
scissors škare f pl
scoop: one/two scoop(s) (of ice cream) jedna kuglica/dvije kuglice
scooter skuter m
scotch (whisky) whisky m
Scotland Škotska f
Scottish škotski
scuba diving ronjenje s aparatom za disanje n
sea more n
seafood plodovi mora m pl
seasick: to be seasick imati morsku bolest
seaside: at the seaside na moru
seaside resort ljetovalište na moru n
season sezona f; (part of year) godišnje doba n
seat sjedište n
sea view pogled na more m
seaweed morska trava f
second drugi
secondary school srednja škola f
second class drugi razred m
second-hand polovan m, polovna f
secure (v) štititi
security sigurnost f
see vidjeti (vidim); **see you later!** vidimo se kasnije!; **see you soon!** do skorog viđenja!; **see you tomorrow!** vidimo se

sutra!
seem činiti se, izgledati; **it seems that …** čini se …
seldom rijetko
self-confidence samopouzdanje n
sell prodavati (prodajem) **78**
Sellotape® selotejp m
send slati (šaljem)
sender pošiljatelj m
sensitive osjetljiv
sentence rečenica f
separate (v) odvojiti
separately odvojen
September rujan m
serious ozbiljan m, ozbiljna f
several nekolicina
sex spol m
shade sjena f; **in the shade** u sjeni
shame sramota f
shampoo šampon m
shape oblik m
share dijeliti
shave brijati se (brijem se)
shaving cream krema za brijanje f
shaving foam pjena za brijanje f
she ona (see grammar)
sheet plahta f
shellfish školjka f
shirt košulja f
shock šok m
shocking šokantan m, šokantna f
shoes cipele f pl
shop dućan m, trgovina f
shop assistant trgovački pomoćnik m, trgovačka pomoćnica f
shopkeeper trgovac m

shopping: to do some/the shopping ići u kupovinu

shopping centre opskrbni centar *m*

short kratak *m*, kratka *f*; **I'm two … short** nedostaju mi dva/dvije ...

short cut prečica *f*

shorts kratke hlačice *f pl*

short-sleeved kratkih rukava

shoulder rame *n*

show *(noun)* predstava *f* **60**

show *(v)* pokazati (pokažem)

shower tuš *m*; **to take a shower** tuširati se

shower gel gel za tuširanje *m*

shut *(v)* zatvoriti

shy plah, sramežljiv

sick: to feel sick osjećati mučninu

side strana *f*

sign *(noun)* znak *m*

sign *(v)* potpisati (potpišem)

signal signal *m* **99**

silent šutljiv

silver srebro *n*

silver-plated posrebren

since od + *gen*

sing pjevati

singer pjevač *m*, pjevačica *f*

single (ticket) karta u jednom smjeru *f*

sister sestra *f*

sit down sjesti (sjednem)

size veličina *f* **82**

ski *(noun)* skija *f*

ski *(v)* skijati se

ski boots pancerice *f pl*

skiing skijanje *n*; **to go skiing** ići na skijanje/skijati

ski lift žičara *f*

skin koža *f*

ski pole skijaški štap *m*

ski resort skijalište *n*

skirt suknja *f*

sky nebo *n*

skyscraper neboder *m*

sleep *(noun)* spavanje *n*

sleep *(v)* spavati; **to sleep with** spavati s

sleeping bag vreća za spavanje *f*

sleeping pill tableta za spavanje *f*

sleepy pospan

sleeve rukav *m*

slice kriška *f*

sliced narezan

slide tobogan *m*; *(photographic)* dijapozitiv *m*

slow spor

slowly polagano

small malen

smell *(noun)* miris *m*

smell *(v)* mirisati (mirišem); **to smell good/bad** ugodno mirisati/zaudarati

smile *(noun)* smiješak *m*

smile *(v)* smiješiti se

smoke *(noun)* dim *m*

smoke *(v)* pušiti

smoker pušač *m*

snack laki obrok *m*, zakuska na brzaka *f*

snow *(noun)* snijeg *m*

snow *(v)* snježiti

so tako; **so that** tako da

soap sapun *m*

soccer nogomet *m*

socks kratke čarape *f pl*

some: some people neki ljudi

somebody, someone netko

something nešto; **something else** nešto drugo

sometimes katkada

somewhere negdje; **somewhere else** negdje drugdje

son sin *m*

song pjesma *f*

soon brzo

sore: to have a sore throat imati grlobolju; **to have a sore head** imati glavobolju

sorry oprostite; **sorry!** ispričavam se!

south jug *m*; **in the south** na jugu; **(to the) south of** južno od

souvenir suvenir *m*

Spain Španjolska *f*

Spanish španjolski

spare pričuva

spare part pričuvni dio *m*

spare tyre pričuvna guma *f*

spare wheel pričuvni kotač *m*

spark plug svijećica *f*

speak govoriti **8**, **10**, **97**, **98**, **109**

special poseban *m*, posebna *f*; **today's special** dnevni specijalitet *m* **46**

speciality specijalnost *f*, specijalitet *m*

speed brzina *f*; **at full speed** punom brzinom

spell pisati slovo po slovo; **how do you spell it?** kako to pišete?

spend trošiti

spice začin *m*

spicy ljut

spider pauk *m*

splinter špranja *f*

split up razdvojiti se

spoil razmaziti

sponge spužva *f*

spoon žlica *f*

sport šport *m*

sports ground športski teren *m*

sporty športski

spot bubuljica *f*

sprain: to sprain one's ankle uganuti gležanj

spring proljeće *n*

square trg *m*

stadium stadion *m*

stain mrlja *f*

stained-glass windows vitraži *m pl*

stairs stepenice *f pl*

stamp poštanska marka *f* **92**

start *(noun)* početak *m*

start *(v)* početi

state država *f*

statement izjava *f*

station kolodvor *m*

stay *(noun)* boravak *m*

stay *(v)* ostajati (ostajem); **to stay in touch** ostati u kontaktu

steal ukrasti (ukradem) **109**

step *(stair)* stuba *f*

sticking plaster flaster *m*

still miran *m*, mirna *f*

still water negazirana voda *f*

sting *(n)* žaoka *f*

sting *(v)* ubosti; **to get stung (by)** uboo me **103**

stock: out of stock rasprodan

stomach trbuh *m*

stone kamen *m*

stop *(noun)* postaja *f* **28**

stop (v) zaustaviti
stopcock pipa f
storey kat m
storm oluja f
straight ahead, straight on ravno
strange čudan m, čudna f
street ulica f
strong jak
stuck zaglavljen
student student m, studentica f **23**
studies studije f pl
study studirati; **to study biology** studirati biologiju
style stil m
subtitled titlovan
suburb predgrađe n
suffer patiti
suggest predlagati (predlažem)
suit: does that suit you? da li vam to odgovara?
suitcase kofer m **25**
summer ljeto n
summit vrh m
sun sunce n; **in the sun** na suncu
sunbathe sunčati se
sunburnt: to get sunburnt izgorjeti na suncu
sun cream krema za sunčanje f
Sunday nedjelja f
sunglasses sunčane naočale f pl
sunhat šešir za sunčanje m
sunrise izlazak sunca m
sunset zalazak sunca m
sunstroke sunčanica f; **to get sunstroke** dobiti sunčanicu
supermarket samoposluživanje n **40**, **78**
supplement dodatak m

sure siguran m, sigurna f
surf surf m
surfboard daska za surfanje f
surfing jahanje na valovima n; **to go surfing** ići surfati
surgical spirit alkohol m
surname prezime n
surprise (noun) iznenađenje n
surprise (v) iznenaditi
sweat znoj m
sweater vesta f
sweet (noun) slatkiš m
sweet (adj) sladak m, slatka f
swim (noun) **to go for a swim** ići plivati
swim (v) plivati
swimming plivanje n
swimming pool bazen za plivanje m
swimming trunks kupaće gaće f pl
swimsuit kupaći kostim m
switch off ugasiti
switch on upaliti
switchboard operator uposlenik m, uposlenica f na centrali
swollen otečen
synagogue sinagoga f
syrup sirup m

T

table stol m **45**
tablespoon žlica f
tablet tableta f
take uzimati; **it takes two hours** to traje dva sata
takeaway hrana za van f
take off (plane) uzletjeti (uzletim)

talk govoriti

tall visok

tampon tampon *m*

tan *(v)* preplanuti (preplanem)

tanned preplanuo *m*, preplanula *f*

tap pipa *f*

taste *(noun)* okus *m*

taste *(v)* kušati

tax porez

tax-free oslobođen od poreza

taxi taxi *m* **31**

taxi driver taxi vozač *m*

T-bar sidro *n* (skijaška žičara)

team tim *m*, momčad *f*

teaspoon žličica *f*

teenager tinejđer *m*

telephone *(noun)* telefon *m*

telephone *(v)* telefonirati

television televizija *f*

tell kazati (kažem)

temperature temperatura *f*; **to take one's temperature** izmjeriti temperaturu

temple hram *m*

temporary privremen

tennis tenis *m*

tennis court tenisko igralište *n*

tennis shoe tenisica *f*

tent šator *m*

tent peg šatorski kočić *m*

terminal terminal *m*

terrace terasa *f*

terrible strašan *m*, strašna *f*

thank zahvaljivati (zahvaljujem); **thank you** hvala vam; **thank you very much** puno vam hvala

thanks hvala; **thanks to** zahvaljujući + *dat*

that taj; **that one** taj

the *(see grammar)*

theatre kazalište *n*

theft krađa *f*

their, theirs njihov

them *(see grammar)*

theme park tematski park *m*

then tada

there tamo; **there is** ima, postoji; **there are** postoje

therefore zbog toga

thermometer toplomjer *m*

Thermos® flask termos boca *f*

these ovi; **these ones** ovi

they oni; **they say that ...** oni kažu kako/da ...

thief lopov *m*

thigh bedro *n*

thin mršav

thing stvar *f*; **things** stvari *pl*

think misliti

think about razmisliti o + *loc*

thirst žeđ *f*

thirsty: to be thirsty biti žedan

this ovaj; **this one** ovaj; **this evening** večeras; **this is** ovo je **14**

those taj; **those ones** ti

throat grlo *n*

throw bacati

throw out izbaciti

Thursday četvrtak *m*

ticket ulaznica *f*, karta *f* **23, 60, 61**

ticket office blagajna *f*

tidy uredan *m*, uredna *f*

tie kravata *f*

tight tijesan *m*, tijesna *f*

tights hula-hupke *f pl*

time vrijeme *n* **117**; **what time**

is it? koliko je sati; **from time to time** s vremena na vrijeme; **on time** na vrijeme; **three/four times** tri/četiri puta

time difference vremenska razlika f

timetable vozni red m **23**

tinfoil alufolija f

tip napojnica f

tired umoran m, umorna f

tobacco duhan m

tobacconist's trafika f

today danas

together zajedno

toilet WC m **8**, **44**

toilet bag toaletna torbica f

toilet paper WC papir m

toiletries toaletne potrepštine f pl

toll cestarina f

tomorrow sutra; **tomorrow evening** sutra navečer; **tomorrow morning** sutra ujutro

tongue jezik m

tonight večeras

too previše; **too bad** šteta; **too many, too much** previše

tooth zub m

toothbrush kefica za zube f

toothpaste pasta za zube f

top vrh m; **at the top** na vrhu

torch baterijska svjetiljka f

touch dodirivati (dodirujem)

tourist turist m

tourist office turistički ured m **65**

towards prema + dat

towel ručnik m

town grad m

town centre centar grada m

town hall vijećnica f, gradsko poglavarstvo n

toy igračka f

traditional tradicionalan m, tradicionalna f

traffic promet m

traffic jam prometna gužva f

train vlak m **28**; **the train to Zagreb** vlak do Zagreba

train station kolodvor m

tram tramvaj m

transfer (of money) doznačivanje novca

translate prevoditi

travel agency putnička agencija f

travel putovanje n

traveller's cheque putnički ček m

trip put m; **have a good trip!** sretan put!

trolley kolica f

trouble: to have trouble doing something imati potočkoća radeći nešto

trousers hlače f pl

true istinit; **it's true** istina je

try pokušati; **to try to do something** pokušati učiniti nešto

try on isprobati

Tuesday utorak m

turn (noun) **it's your turn** vi ste/ti si na redu

turn (v) okretati (okrećem)

twice dva puta

type (noun) vrsta f

type (v) tipkati

typical tipičan m, tipična f

tyre guma f

umbrella kišobran *m*
uncomfortable neudoban *m*, neudobna *f*
under ispod + *gen*
underneath ispod
understand razumjeti **10**
underwear donje rublje *n*
United Kingdom Velika Britanija *f*
United States Sjedinjene Američke Države *f pl*
until sve do + *gen*
upset uznemiren
upstairs gore, na katu
urgent žuran *m*, žurna *f*
us *(see grammar)*
use: to be used for biti uporabljen za; **I'm used to it** navikao/kla sam na to
useful koristan *m*, korisna *f*
useless nesposoban *m*, nesposobna *f*
usually obično
U-turn zaokret unazad *m*

vaccinated (against) cijepljen/ cijepljena (protiv)
valid (for) vrijedan (za)
valid punovrijedan *m*, punovrijedna *f*
valley dolina *f*
VAT PDV *m*
vegetarian vegetarijanac *m*, vegetarijanka *f*
very vrlo
view pogled *m*

villa vila *f*
village selo *n*
visa viza *f*
visit *(noun)* posjet *m*
visit *(v)* posjetiti
volleyball odbojka *f*
vomit povraćati

waist struk *m*
wait čekati; **to wait for someone/something** čekati nekoga/nešto
waiter konobar *m*
waitress konobarica *f*
wake up probuditi se
Wales Wales *m*
walk *(noun)* **to go for a walk** ići u šetnju **72**, **73**
walk *(v)* šetati
walking: to go walking ići u šetnju/ići hodati
walking boots gojzerice *f pl*
Walkman® Walkman *m*
wallet novčanik *m*
want htjeti (hoću); **to want to do something** htjeti učiniti nešto
warm topao *m*, topla *f*
warn upozoriti
wash *(noun)* **to have a wash** prati se (perem se)
wash *(v)* prati (perem); **to wash one's hair** prati kosu
washbasin umivaonik *m*
washing: to do the washing prati rublje
washing machine perilica *f*
washing powder deterdžent *m*
washing-up liquid deterdžent

za pranje suđa *m*
wasp osa *f*
watch *(noun)* ura *f*
watch *(v)* gledati; **watch out!** pazi!
water voda *f* **46**, **47**
water heater grijač za vodu *m*, bojler *m*
waterproof nepromočiv
waterskiing skijanje na vodi *n*
wave val *m*
way put *m*
way in ulaz *m*
way out izlaz *m*
we mi
weak slab
wear odijevati se
weather vrijeme *n* **21**; **the weather's bad** vrijeme je loše
weather forecast vremenska prognoza *f* **20**
website web stranica *f*
Wednesday srijeda *f*
week tjedan *m*
weekend vikend *m*
welcome dobrodošlica *f*; **welcome!** dobrodošli!; **you're welcome** nema na čemu
well dobro; **I'm very well** ja sam jako dobro; **well done** *(meat)* dobro pečen
well-known poznat
Welsh velški
west zapad *m*; **in the west** na zapadu; **(to the) west of** zapadno od
wet mokar *m*, mokra *f*
wetsuit ronilačko odijelo *n*
what što; **what do you want?** što želite?

wheel kotač *m*
wheelchair invalidska kolica *f*
when kada
where gdje; **where is/are …?** gdje je/su …?; **where are you from?** odakle ste?; **where are you going?** kamo idete?
which koji
while dok
white bijel
white wine bijelo vino *n*
who tko; **who's calling?** tko zove?
whole cijeli; **the whole cake** cijeli kolač
whose čiji
why zašto
wide širok
wife supruga *f*
wild divlji
wind vjetar *m*
window prozor *m*; **in the window** u izlogu
windscreen vjetrobran *m*
windsurfing surfanje s jedrom *m*
wine vino *n* **47**, **48**
winter zima *f*
with s, sa + *inst*
withdraw povući (povučem)
without bez + *gen*
woman žena *f*
wonderful čudesan *m*, čudesna *f*
wood drvo *n*
wool vuna *f*
work *(noun)* rad *m*, djelo *n*; **work of art** umjetničko djelo *n*
work *(v)* raditi **15**
works radovi *m pl*
world svijet *m*

worse gore, lošije; **to get worse** osjećati se lošije; **it's worse (than)** lošije je nego
worth: to be worth vrijediti; **it's worth it** to i vrijedi toliko
wound rana f
wrist zglavak m
write pisati (pišem) **10**, **80**
wrong pogrešan m, pogrešna f

year godina f
yellow žut
yes da
yesterday jučer; **yesterday evening** jučer navečer
you ti/vi
young mlad
your, yours tvoj/vaš
youth hostel omladinski hotel m

XYZ

X-rays rendgen m

zero ništica f
zip patentni zatvarač m
zoo zoološki vrt m
zoom (lens) zum m

DICTIONARY

CROATIAN-ENGLISH

A

adapter adaptor
adresa address
ako if
akumulator battery
alergičan, alergična allergic
ali but
alkohol alcohol, surgical spirit
alufolija tinfoil
američki American *(adj)*
Amerikanac, Amerikanka
  American *(noun)*
anestetik anaesthetic
antibiotici antibiotics
aroma flavour
aspirin aspirin
astma asthma
autobus bus, coach
autobusna linija bus route
autobusna postaja bus stop
autobusni kolodvor bus station
autocesta motorway
automatska sekretarica
  answering machine
automobil car
autostopiranje hitchhiking
autostopirati to hitchhike
avenija avenue
avion *m* plane

B

bacati to throw
balkon balcony
banka bank
bankomat cashpoint
bar bar
baterijska svjetiljka torch
bazen za plivanje swimming pool
beba baby
bedro thigh
Belgija Belgium
Belgijanac, Belgijanka Belgian
  (noun)
belgijski Belgian *(adj)*
benzinska crpka petrol station
bez + *gen* without
bezopasan, bezopasna safe
bicikl bicycle
biciklistička staza cycle path
bijel white
bijelo vino white wine
biljka plant
biti *(see grammar)* to be
bivši former
blagajna checkout, ticket office
blizu + *gen* near
bljeskalica flash *(on camera)*
boca bottle
bočica baby's bottle
boja colour, paint
bok! hi!, bye!
bolest illness

bolestan, bolesna ill
bolnica hospital
bolji better
boravak stay *(noun)*
botanički vrt botanical garden
bova buoy
brada beard, chin
branik bumper
brat brother
brava lock
brdo hill
brdski bicikl mountain bike
brijač razor
brijati se (brijem se) to shave
brinuti o to look after, to worry about
brod boat
broj number
brojati (brojim) to count
brojilo indicator
bronhitis bronchitis
brošura brochure
brz fast, quick
brzina speed
brzo quickly, soon
bubreg kidney
bubuljica spot
bučan, bučna noisy
budilica alarm clock
buka noise

C

carinarnica customs
CD CD
centar centre
centar grada town centre
centimetar centimetre
cesta road
cestarina toll

cigara cigar
cigareta cigarette
cijeli all, whole
cijena cost, price
cijena vožnje fare
cijepljen: biti cijepljen (protiv) to be vaccinated (against)
cipele shoes
cirkus circus
Coca Cola Coke®
crijevna gripa gastric flu
crkva church
crn black
crno vino red wine
crta line
crven red
crveno svjetlo red light
curiti to leak

Č

časopis magazine
čaša glass
ček cheque
čekati u redu to queue
čekati to wait, to wait for
čelo forehead
čepići za uši earplugs
često often
češalj comb
četka brush
četvrtak Thursday
četvrtina quarter
čiji whose
činiti to do, to make
činiti se to seem
činjenica fact
čist clean
čistiti to clean
čitati to read

član member
čudan, čudna strange
čudesan, čudesna wonderful
čuti (čujem) to hear
čuvati to keep, to look after
čvoruga bump

D

da yes
dakako of course
dalek far
dan day
danas today
dan danas nowadays
dar present
daska za surfanje surfboard
datum date
datum rođenja date of birth
davati (dajem) to give
desert dessert
desni right *(adj)*
deterdžent washing powder
deterdžent za pranje suđa washing-up liquid
devizni tečaj exchange rate
dezinficirati to disinfect
dezodorans deodorant
dežurna ljekarna duty chemist's
digitalna kamera digital camera
dijeliti to share
dijeta diet
dijete child
dim smoke
dimnjak chimney
dio part
disko disco
divlji wild
dizalo lift
dizel diesel

dječja kolica pram
djevojačko prezime maiden name
djevojka girl, girlfriend
dnevna soba living room
dno bottom
dob age
dobar, dobra good, fine
dobivati to get
dobra *(n)* goods
dobre: biti dobre volje to be in a good mood
dobro well
dobrodošao, dobrodošla welcome
dodatak supplement
dodatan, dodatna extra
dodirivati (dodirujem) to touch
dogoditi se to happen
dok while
dokumenti identity papers
dolazak arrival
dolaziti to arrive, to come
dolina valley
dolje downstairs
dom home
donje rublje underwear
donositi to bring
doručak breakfast
dosegnuti to reach
dosta enough
dostupan, dostupna available
doticaj contact
dovesti (dovedem) to fetch *(person)*
doviđenja! goodbye!
doznačivanje novca transfer *(of money)*
dozvoliti to allow
drag dear
drago mi je pleased to meet you
drijemati to doze

drugi second, other
drugi razred second class
drvo wood
držati (držim) to hold
država state
državni blagdan national holiday
dubok deep
dućan shop
dug long
dugovati (dugujem) to owe
duhan tobacco
dva puta twice
dvogled binoculars
dvorac castle, palace

DŽ

džamija mosque
džemper jumper

E

električni electric
električni brijač electric shaver
e-mail e-mail
e-mail adresa e-mail address
Engleska England
engleski English
epileptičar epileptic
Euroček Eurocheque
Europa Europe
Europljanin, Europljanka European *(noun)*
europski European *(adj)*
euro super 95 four-star petrol

F

faks fax
far headlight

fast food restoran fast-food restaurant
festival festival
film film, movie
flaster Elastoplast®, sticking plaster
fotoaparat camera
fotografija photo
Francuska France
francuski French
frizer, frizerka hairdresser
funta pound

G

galerija gallery
garancija guarantee
garaža garage
garderoba left-luggage (office)
gaza gauze
gaziran fizzy
gdje where
gel za tuširanje shower gel
ginekolog, ginekologinja gynaecologist
gips plaster (cast)
glačalo iron
glačati to iron
glad hunger
gladan, gladna to be hungry
glasan loud
glava head
glavni main
glavno jelo main course
glavobolju: imati glavobolju to have a headache
glazba music
gledati to look, to look at, to watch
gležanj ankle
globa fine *(n)*

gluh deaf
gluten: ne sadrži gluten gluten-free
godina year
godišnjica anniversary
gojzerice walking boots
gol naked
gore *(adj)* worse
gore *(adv)* upstairs
gorivo petrol
gospodin Mr
gospođa Mrs
gospođica Miss
gost guest
gostionica guest house
gotovina cash
govoriti to speak, talk
grad town
graditi to build
gram gram
Grčka Greece
grčki Greek *(adj)*
grijač za vodu water heater
grijanje heating
gripa flu
gristi (grizem) to bite
Grk, Grkinja Greek *(noun)*
grlo throat; **imati grlobolju** to have a sore throat
groblje cemetery
grudnjak bra
gubitak svijesti blackout
guliti to peel
guma tyre
gurni! push!

H

halo hello
hašiš hashish

hemeroidi piles
hi-fi hi-fi
hitan slučaj emergency
hlače trousers, pants
hladan, hladna cold
hladnoća cold *(noun)*
hladnjak fridge
hodati: ići hodati to go walking
Holandija Holland
homoseksualan homosexual, gay *(adj)*
hram temple
hrana food
hrana za van takeaway
htjeti (hoću) to want
hula-hupke tights
hvala thanks

I

i and
iako although
ići (idem) to go; **ići s** *(+ instr)* to go with
igra game
igračka toy
igrati se to play
ili or
imati to have
ime name
imenik directory
inače otherwise
infekcija infection
inozeman, inozemna foreign
inozemstvo: u inozemstvu abroad
insekt insect
insekticid insecticide
instant kava instant coffee
Internet Internet

Internet cafe Internet café
invalidna osoba disabled
invalidska kolica wheelchair
injekcija injection
irski Irish
Irska Ireland
iscrpljen exhausted
iscrpljenost exhaustion
iskrcati se to get off *(boat)*
ispod underneath, below, under
ispričati se to excuse oneself
isprika excuse *(noun)*
isprobati to try on
ispušna cijev exhaust pipe
isti same
istinit true
istok east
išta anything
Italija Italy
iza + *gen* behind
izbaciti to throw out
izgled to appear
izgorjeti na suncu to get
  sunburnt
izgubiti to lose
izjava statement
izlaz exit, gate, way out
izlazak sunca sunrise
izlaziti to come out, to go out
izlaz u slučaju nužde emergency
  exit
izložba exhibition
između + *gen* between, among
iznad + *gen* above
iznad dopuštene težine
  overweight
iznenaditi to surprise
iznenađenje surprise *(noun)*
iznijeti (iznesem) to put out, to
  take out

izravan, izravna direct
izuzetan, izuzetna exceptional
izuzev except

ja I
jahanje na valovima surfing
jak strong
jakna jacket
japanke flip-flops
jastučnica pillowcase
jastuk pillow
javni blagdan public holiday
javnost public
jedan, jedna one
jedanput once
jednako equally
**jednokratnu: za jednokratnu
  uporabu** disposable
jedrenje sailing
jedro sail
jeftin cheap
jelo dish
jelovnik menu
jer because
jesen autumn
jesti (jedem) to eat
jetra liver
jezero lake
jezik language, tongue
još jedan another
jučer yesterday
jug south
jutro morning

kabina za presvlačenje changing
  room, fitting room

kaciga helmet
kada *(adv)* when
kada *(noun)* bath
kafić café
kajak kayak
kako how
kakvoća quality
kamen stone
kamion lorry
kamp campsite
kampiranje camping
kampist camper
kanta za smeće bin, dustbin
kao as
kapelica chapel
kapi drops
karta ticket, map
karta u jednom smjeru single ticket
kartica tekućeg računa debit card
kasko osiguranje comprehensive insurance
kasni late
kasniti to be delayed
kašalj cough *(noun)*
kašljati to cough
kat floor, storey
katastrofa disaster
katedrala cathedral
katkada sometimes
kava coffee
kazališna predstava play, performance
kazalište theatre
kazati (kažem) to say, to tell
kćer daughter
kefica za zube toothbrush
kemijska čistionica dry cleaner's
kilometar kilometre

kinematograf cinema
kiša rain
kišiti to rain
kišni ogrtač raincoat
kišobran umbrella
klima climate
klima uređaj air conditioning
ključ key
knjiga book *(noun)*
knjižara bookshop
knjižnica library
kocka leda ice cube
kočiti to brake
kočnica brake *(noun)*
kod + *gen* by, at
kofer suitcase
koje vrste ...? what kind of ...?
koji which
kolekcija collection
kolica pushchair, trolley
koljeno knee
kolodvor station
kolovoz August
komad piece
komadić bit
komarac mosquito
kompanija company
kompjuter computer
konačno finally
koncert concert
koncertna dvorana concert hall
konobar waiter
konobarica waitress
kontaktne leće contact lenses
kontrola check
konzerva can
konj horse
koristan, korisna useful
kosa hair
košulja shirt

kotač wheel
koturaljke rollerblades
koža skin
krađa theft
kraj end
krajobraz scenery
krajolik landscape
kratak, kratka short
kratke čarape socks
kratke hlačice shorts
kratkih rukava short-sleeved
kravata tie
kreditna kartica credit card
krema za brijanje shaving cream
krema za lice moisturizer
krema za poslije sunčanja
  after-sun (cream)
krema za sunčanje sun cream
krevet bed
kriška slice
križ cross *(noun)*
krpa za suđe dish towel
krpica za pranje lica facecloth
kruh bread
kružni tok roundabout
kružno putovanje cruise
krv blood
krvariti to bleed
krvni tlak blood pressure
kuća house
kuglica scoop *(of ice cream)*
kuhalo za kampiranje camping
  stove
kuhan cooked
kuhar, kuharica cook
kuhati to cook
kuhinja kitchen
kuk hip
kupaće gaće swimming trunks
kupaći kostim swimsuit

kupaonica bathroom
kupovanje shopping
kupovati (kupujem) to buy
kušati to taste
kuverta envelope
kvačilo clutch
kvar na automobilu breakdown
kvaru: u kvaru out of order

L

lagan easy, light
laki obrok snack
laku noć goodnight
leća lens
led ice
leđa back
let flight
letak leaflet
letjeti (letim) to fly
lice face
liječnik, liječnica doctor
liječnik opće prakse GP
lijek medicine
lijekovi drugs
lijep beautiful
lijevi left
lipanj June
listopad October
litica cliff
litra litre
lokalno vrijeme local time
lom fracture
lomljiv fragile
lonac pot, saucepan
lopov thief
loš bad
luka port
luksuz luxury *(noun)*
luksuzan, luksuzna luxury *(adj)*

LJ

ljekarna chemist's
ljeto summer
ljetovalište holiday camp
ljetovalište na moru seaside resort
ljubičast purple
ljudi people
ljut spicy

M

madrac mattress
majka mother
malen little, small
malo little *(adv)*
mamurluk hangover
manastir monastery
manje less
mast ointment
mastan, masna fat
materijal material
medeni mjesec honeymoon
medicinska sestra nurse
međunarodni international
međunarodni platni nalog international money order
menadžer manager
mesnica butcher's
metar metre
metnuti (metnem) to put
mi we
mijenjati to exchange
mikrovalna pećnica microwave
mineralna voda mineral water
minuta minute
miran, mirna quiet, still
miris smell *(noun)*
mirisati (mirišem) to smell

misa mass
misliti to think
miš mouse
mišić muscle
mišljenje opinion
mjenjač gearbox
mjerilo meter
mjerilo za struju electricity meter
mjesec month, moon
mjesečnica period
mjesto place
mlad young
mlak lukewarm
mlin mill
mnogo a lot (of), much
mobitel mobile (phone)
moći (mogu, možeš) to be able to
moguć possible
moj my, mine
mokar, mokra wet
molim please
morati to have to
more sea
morska trava seaweed
morsko: imati morsku bolest to be seasick
most bridge
motorkotač motorbike
možda maybe
mrav ant
mrlja stain
mršav thin
mrtav, mrtva dead
mrziti to hate
muha fly *(noun)*
muškarac man
muški WC gents' (toilet)
muzej museum

na + *loc* on; **na moru** at the seaside; **na katu** upstairs
naći (nađem) to find
nadoknaditi to refund
nagrada prize
najam rental
najbolji best
najmanje least
najvjerojatnije probably
nakit jewellery
naknada refund *(noun)*
nalikovati to look like
namjeravati to intend to
namjerno on purpose
naočale glasses
napadati to attack
naplaćivati (naplaćujem) to charge
napojnica tip
napuniti rezervoar benzinom to fill up with petrol
naranča orange
narezan sliced
naručiti to order
narudžba order *(of food)*
nas us *(see grammar)*
nasumce at random
naš our, ours
naušnice earrings
navijač fan *(supporter)*
nazdravlje! bless you!
ne no, not
nebo sky
neboder skyscraper
nedjelja Sunday
negazirana voda still water
negdje somewhere
neki some

nekolicina several
nekoliko few
nemam ništa protiv I don't mind
neophodan, neophodna necessary
nepromočiv waterproof
nepušač non-smoker
nesanica insomnia
nesposoban, nesposobna useless
nesreća accident
nešto something
netko somebody, someone
neudata single man, single woman
neudoban, neudobna uncomfortable
nezavisan, nezavisna independent
ni neither, nor
nigdje nowhere
nije bitno it doesn't matter
nijedan, nijedna none
Nijemac German *(n)*
nikada never
niski krvni tlak low blood pressure
niskokaloričan low-fat
ništa nothing
ništica zero
nitko nobody, no one
nizak, niska low
Nizozemska Netherlands
noć night
noćni klub nightclub
noga foot, leg
nogomet soccer
nokat nail
nos nose
nositi to carry
notes notebook

nov new
novac money
Nova godina New Year
novčanica banknote
novčanik purse, wallet
novčić coin
novinarnica newsstand
novine newspaper
nož knife

NJ

njegov his
Njemačka Germany
njemački German *(adj)*
Njemica German *(noun)*
njezin her, hers
njihov their, theirs

O

o + *loc* about
oba both
obala coast
obavijest information
obećati to promise
obično usually
obitelj family
objed lunch
oblik shape
obrok meal
ocean ocean
oči eyes
očigledan, očigledna obvious
od + *gen* from, of, since
odbiti to refuse
odbojka volleyball
odgovarati to answer
odgovor answer *(noun)*
odijevati se to dress

odjeća clothes
odjel department
odjeljak compartment
odjenuti se to get dressed
odlazak departure
odlaziti to go away
odmah immediately
odmarati se to rest
odmor holiday(s)
odvjetnik, odvjetnica lawyer
odvojeno separately
odvojiti to separate
oglasnik listings magazine
oko + *gen (prep)* around
oko *(noun)* eye
okretati (okrećem) to turn
okrugao, okrugla round
okus taste
olovka pencil
oluja storm
omiljen favourite
omladinski hotel youth hostel
on he
ona she
onesvijestiti se to faint
oni they
ono it
opasan, opasna dangerous
opatija abbey
opći general
opeći (opečem) to burn
opeklina burn *(noun)*
operaciju: imati operaciju to
have an operation
oprema equipment
oprostite sorry, I beg your pardon
opskrbni centar shopping centre
optičar, optičarka optician
organizirati to organize
organski organic

orkestar orchestra
osa wasp
oseka low tide
osigurač fuse
osiguranje insurance
osjećaj feeling
osjećati se to feel; **osjećati mučninu** to feel sick
osjetljiv sensitive
oslobođen od poreza tax-free
osnova basis
osoba person
osobna iskaznica identity card
osobni stereo personal stereo
ostajati (ostajem) to stay
ostatak remainder
ostati bez benzina to run out of petrol
ostaviti to leave
oštećen damaged
otac father
otečen swollen
otkazivati (otkazujem) to cancel
otok island
otvarač za boce bottle opener
otvarač za konzerve can opener
otvoren open *(adj)*
otvoriti to open
ovaj this
ovdje here
ovi these
ozbiljan, ozbiljna serious
ozlijeđen injured
ožujak March

P

pacijent patient
padati to fall
paket aranžman package holiday

pakirati to pack
pamuk cotton
pancerice ski boots
pansion full board
papa! bye!
papir paper; **papir za zamotavanje poklona** gift-wrap
par pair
parfem perfume
parkiralište car park, parking space
parkirati to park
pasta za zube toothpaste
patentni zatvarač zip
patiti to suffer
pauk spider
pčela bee
PDV VAT
peći (pečem) to bake
pećnica oven
pekara baker's
pelena nappy
peludna groznica hay fever
penjanje climbing
pepeljara ashtray
perfektan perfect
perilica washing machine
perilica za suđe dishwasher
pero pen
peron platform
petak Friday
piće drink *(noun)*
pijan drunk
pijesak sand
piknik picnic
pilula pill; **uzimati pilulu** to be on the pill
pilula za dan poslije morning-after pill
PIN PIN (number)

pipa stopcock, tap
pisati (pišem) to write
pisati slovo po slovo to spell
pismo letter
piškiti to pee
pita pie
pitanje question
pitati to ask
piti (pijem) to drink
pitka voda drinking water
pjena za brijanje shaving foam
pjesma song, poem
pješačka zona pedestrianized street
pješak pedestrian
pjevač, pjevačica singer
pjevati to sing
plah shy
plahta sheet
plak hotplate
plakati (plačem) to cry
plan plan, map
planina mountain
planinarenje hill-walking
planinarska koliba mountain hut
plastična vrećica plastic bag
plastika plastic
platiti to pay
plav blue
plaža beach
ples dance *(noun)*
plesati (plešem) to dance
plik blister
plima high tide
plin gas
plinska svjetiljka gas cylinder
plivanje swimming
plivati to swim; **ići plivati** to go for a swim
plodovi mora seafood

plomba filling *(in tooth)*
pljačka rip-off
pluća lungs
početak beginning
početi (počnem) to begin
početnik, početnica beginner
poderotina flaw
podne midday
podnositi to put up with
područje area
podsjetiti to remind
pogled view
pogled na more sea view
pogrešan, pogrešna wrong
pogreška mistake
pokazati (pokažem) to show
pokrivač blanket, cover
pokrivati to cover
pokušati to try
pokvariti to spoil
pola half; **pola pinte** half-pint
polagano slowly
polazak departure
policajac policeman
policajka police woman
policija police
policijska postaja police station
polog deposit
polovan second-hand
polupansion half-board
pomagati (pomažem) to help
pomoć help *(noun)*
ponedjeljak Monday
ponoć midnight
ponosan, ponosna (na + *acc*) proud (of)
ponoviti to repeat
ponovno again
ponovno otvoriti to reopen
ponuda offer

popravljati to repair
popuniti to fill in, to fill out
popust discount
porez tax
portret portrait
Portugal Portugal
Portugalac, Portugalka
 Portuguese *(noun)*
portugalski Portuguese *(adj)*
poruka message
posao job
poseban, posebna special
posjedovati (posjedujem) to own
posjet visit
posjetiti to visit
poslanstvo consulate
poslije later, past
poslije + *gen* after
poslijepodne afternoon
pospan sleepy
posrebren silver-plated
postaja (bus) stop
postotak percent
posuditi to borrow, to lend
posve completely, quite
posvuda everywhere
pošiljatelj sender
pošta post, post office
poštanska dopisnica postcard
poštanska marka stamp
poštanska pošiljka packet, parcel
poštanske pošiljke mail
poštanski broj postcode
poštanski sandučić postbox
poštanski ured post office
poštar postman
pošten honest
poteškoća: imati poteškoća
 radeći nešto to have trouble
 doing something

potpisati (potpišem) to sign
potvrda o primitku receipt
potvrđivati (potvrđujem) to
 confirm
povišena temperatura fever
povlastica concession
povlastica na vožnju discount
 fare
povraćati to vomit
povratak return
povratna karta return ticket
povući (povučem) to withdraw
poziv call *(noun)*
poziv na račun nazvanog
 reverse-charge call
pozivati to invite
pozivni broj dialling code
poznat well-known
požuri! hurry (up)!
praktičan, praktična practical
praonica rublja launderette
prati (perem) to wash
prati rublje to do the washing
prati se (perem se) to have a
 wash
pravo right *(noun)*
prazan, prazna empty
prazna guma flat tyre
prečica short cut
predgrađe suburb
predlagati (predlažem) to suggest
predložiti to propose
predmet item
prednji forward *(adj)*
prednji dio front
predstava show *(noun)*
preko + *gen* across
preko puta + *gen* opposite *(prep)*
prekoračenje dozvoljene
 težine excess baggage

prekuhan overdone
prelaziti to cross
prema + *dat* towards
preplanuo tanned
preplanuti (preplanem) to tan
preporučiti to advise, to recommend
prepoznati to recognize
prethodan, prethodna previous
pretrpan crowded, packed
previše too, too much
prevoditi to translate
prezervativ condom
prezime surname
pričekajte trenutak! hold on!
pričuva spare
pričuvna guma spare tyre
pričuvni dio spare part
pričuvni kotač spare wheel
prihvatiti to accept
prijatelj, prijateljica friend
prijaviti to declare
prijaviti boravak u hotelu to check in
prije before
prilično rather
primati to receive
pripaliti to light
prirediti to prepare, to put on
priroda countryside, nature
pristanište quay
pristojba charge *(noun)*
pristup access
pristupnina admission
pritisnuti (pritisnem) to press
privatan, privatna private
privremen temporary
prizemlje ground floor
prljav dirty
probuditi se to wake up

procesija procession
prodavač novina newsagent
prodavati (prodajem) to sell
prognoza forecast
program programme
proizvod product
prolaziti to pass
proljeće spring
proljev: imati proljev to have diarrhoea
promet traffic
prometna gužva traffic jam
prometni znak road sign
propusnica pass *(noun)*
propustiti to miss
prosinac December
prošli last
protiv + *gen* against
prozor window
prsa chest
prst finger
prtljaga baggage, luggage
prtljažnik boot *(of car)*
prvi first
prvi kat first floor
prvi razred first class
pržen fried
puder powder
pumpa za bicikl bicycle pump
pun full
puna cijena full fare, full price
puno lots, many
punovrijedan, punovrijedna valid
pušač smoker
put journey, trip, way
putnička agencija travel agency
putnički ček traveller's cheque
putnik passenger
putovanje travel
putovnica passport

R

raca duck
račun bill
rad work
radijator radiator
radio postaja radio station
raditi to work
radost delight
radovi works
rame shoulder
rana wound
rani early
rasist racist
rasprodaja sale
rasprodan sold out
rasprsnut burst *(adj)*
rasprsnuti se (rasprsnem se) to burst
rasti (rastem) to grow
ravno straight ahead, straight on
razborit reasonable
razdvojiti se to split (up)
različit different
razmaziti to spoil
razmijeniti to change
razmisliti o + *loc* to think about
razumjeti to understand
razviti film to get a film developed
rebro rib
recepcija reception
recepcionist, recepcionistica receptionist
recept recipe
rečenica sentence
red order; **ti si na redu** it's your turn
registracija putnika check-in *(at airport)*
registarske pločice number plates

registriran registered
reket racket
rekreativno pješačenje hiking
rendgen X-ray
rep queue
restoran restaurant
reumatizam rheumatism
rezati (režem) to cut
rezerviran reserved
rezervirati to book, to reserve
riba fish
ribarnica fishmonger's, fish shop
rijedak, rijetka rare
rijeka river
rijetko rarely
rikverc reverse gear
rizik risk
rizle cigarette papers
robna kuća department store
roditelji parents
rođendan birthday
rok isteka valjanosti expiry date
roman novel
ronilačko odijelo wetsuit
roniti to dive
ronjenje: ići na ronjenje to go diving; **ronjenje s aparatom za disanje** scuba diving
roštilj barbecue
ručna kočnica handbrake
ručna prtljaga hand luggage
ručna torbica handbag
ručnik towel
ručnik za kupanje bath towel
ručni rad hand-made
rujan September
ruka arm, hand
rukav sleeve
ruksak backpack, rucksack
rupčić handkerchief

ruševina ruins
ružica rosé wine
ružičast pink

S

s, sa + *inst* with
sačuvati to save
sada now
sajam fair *(noun)*
sam oneself
samo only
samoposluživanje supermarket
samopouzdanje self-confidence
sandale sandals
sandučić za poštu letterbox
sapun soap
sastanak meeting
sat hour
savjet advice
sedežnica chairlift
selo village, country
selotejp Sellotape®
sestra sister
sezona season
sidro T-bar, anchor
siguran, sigurna sure
sigurnosni pojas safety belt
sigurnost safety, security
siječanj January
silovanje rape
sin son
sinagoga synagogue
siromašan, siromašna poor
sirov raw
sirup syrup
sit: biti sit to be full
sitan novac change *(money)*
siv grey
sjećati se to remember

Sjedinjene Američke Države
 United States
sjedaloište seat
sjena shade
sjesti (sjednem) to sit down
sjever north
skija ski
skijalište ski resort
skijanje na vodi waterskiing
skijaški štap ski pole
skijati to ski
skup expensive
skuter scooter
slab weak
sladak, slatka sweet *(adj)*
slan salty
slast: u-slast! enjoy your meal!
slati (šaljem) to send
slatkiš sweet *(noun)*
slijedeći next
slijep blind
slika painting, picture
slobodan, slobodna free
slomltl break
slomljen broken
slučaju: u slučaju + *gen* in case
 of; **u svakom slučaju** in any case
slušati to listen
služba informacija directory
 enquiries
**služba za pomoć na cesti
 (HAK)** breakdown service
smanjiti to reduce
smeće rubbish
smeđ brown
smijati se (smijem se) to laugh
smiješak smile *(noun)*
smiješiti se to smile
smjer direction
smještaj accommodation

snijeg snow
sniženje reduction
snježiti to snow
soba room
sok juice
sol salt
spavačica nightdress
spavanje sleep
spavati to sleep
specijalitet speciality
spirala coil (contraceptive)
spol sex
spomenik monument
spor slow
spreman, spremna ready
spužva sponge
sramota shame
srce heart
srčani udar heart attack
srebro silver
sreća luck
sredina middle
srednja škola secondary school
srednji medium
sredstva za kontracepciju contraceptives
sretan, sretna happy, lucky
srijeda Wednesday
srpanj July
srušiti to knock down
stadion stadium
stambena prikolica caravan
stan flat, apartment
stanarina rent (noun)
star old
stari grad old town
staza path
stepenice stairs
stijena rock
stil style

stol table
stolica chair
stoljeće century
stopalo foot
strana side
stranac, strankinja foreigner
strašan, strašna terrible
stroj engine
struja electricity
stuba step
studen cold (adj)
studeni November
student, studentica student
studije studies
studirati to study
stupanj degree
stupiti u vezu to contact
stvar thing
subota Saturday
suđe dishes
suh dry
suknja skirt
sukob fight
sunce sun
suncobran beach umbrella
sunčane naočale sunglasses
sunčanica sunstroke
sunčati se sunbathe
suprotnost opposite (noun)
suprug husband
supruga wife
surfanje s jedrom windsurfing
susjed, susjeda neighbour
susresti (susretnem) to meet
sušilo za kosu hairdrier
sušiti to dry
sutra tomorrow
suvenir souvenir
suvremen modern
svaki each, every

svatko anybody, anyone
svi everybody, everyone
sve do + *gen* until
svibanj May
svijeća candle
svijećica spark plug
svijet world
svijetli light *(adj)*
svjetiljka lamp
svjetionik lighthouse
svjež cool
svrbi me I've got an itch

Š

šalica cup
šampon shampoo
šator tent
šatorski kočić tent peg
šećerna bolest diabetes
šešir hat
šešir za sunčanje sunhat
šetati to walk
šetnju: ići u šetnju to go for a walk
šibica match *(for fire)*
širok wide
škare scissors
školjka shell, shellfish
škotski Scottish
šok shock
šokantan, šokantna shocking
španjolski Spanish
Španjolska Spain
šport sport
športski sport *(adj)*
športski teren sports ground
špranja splinter
štapići za uši cotton buds
štep-deka ground sheet

šteta je it's a pity
štititi to protect
što what
šuma forest
šutljiv silent

T

tableta tablet
tableta za spavanje sleeping pill
tada then
taj that
tako so
također also
Talijan, Talijanka Italian *(noun)*
talijanski Italian *(adj)*
taman, tamna dark
tamo there; **tamo prijeko** over there
tanjur plate
tava frying pan
taxi vozač taxi driver
tek just
telefon telephone
telefonirati to telephone
telefonska govornica phone box
telefonska kartica phonecard
telefonski broj phone number
telefonski poziv phone call
televizija television
tematski park theme park
temperatura temperature
tenis tennis
tenisica tennis shoe
tenisko igralište tennis court
tepih rug
terasa terrace
teren za golf golf course
termos boca Thermos® flask
težak, teška difficult, heavy

ti those; you
tijekom + *gen* during
tijelo body
tijesan, tijesna tight
tim team
tinejđer teenager
tipičan, tipična typical
tipkati to type
titlovan subtitled
tjedan week
tko who
tlak pressure
to ovisi o + *loc* that depends (on)
toaletna torbica toilet bag
toaletne potrepštine toiletries
tobogan slide
točan, točna correct
točeno pivo draught beer
točka point
topao, topla warm
toplomjer thermometer
torba bag
tradicionalan, tradicionalna traditional
trafika tobacconist's
trajati (trajem) to last, to endure
trajekt ferry
tramvaj tram
trava grass
travanj April
tražiti to look for
trbuh stomach
trebati to need
trenutak moment
trg square
trgovac shopkeeper
trgovački pomoćnik shop assistant
trgovina mješovite robe grocer's

trošiti to spend
trovanje hranom food poisoning
trudna pregnant
tržnica market
turist tourist
turistička klasa economy class
turistički obilazak u pratnji vodiča guided tour
turistički ured tourist office
tuš shower
tužan, tužna sad
tvoj your, yours
tvrd hard

U

u + *loc* at, in
ubiti (ubijem) to kill
ubosti (ubodem) to sting
ubrus napkin
učiti to learn
udaljen distant
udoban, udobna comfortable
uganuti gležanj to sprain one's ankle
ugasiti to switch off
ugovoriti to arrange
ugriz bite *(noun)*
uho ear
uhvatiti to catch
ujak uncle *(mother's brother)*
ukloniti to remove
uključiti to plug in
ukrasti (ukradem) to steal
ukrcaj boarding
ulaz entrance
ulaziti to come in, to go in
ulaznica entry ticket
ulica street
ulijevati (ulijevam) to pour

uložak sanitary towel
ulje oil
umivaonik washbasin
umjesto +gen instead of
umjetnik, umjetnica artist
umjetnost art
umoran, umorna tired
umrijeti to die
unajmiti to hire, to rent
unaprijed in advance
unutra inside
upala slijepog crijeva appendicitis
upaliti to light, to switch on
upaljač lighter
uplašiti se + gen to be scared (of)
uporaba use
uposlenik na centrali switchboard operator
upozoriti to warn
upravljati to operate
ura watch (noun)
uračunat included
uredan, uredna tidy
usitniti to change (money)
Uskrs Easter
usluga favour
usnica lip
usoljen salted
uspjevati to manage
usta mouth
ustajati (ustajem) to get up
uši ears
utikač plug
utopiti se to drown
utorak Tuesday
uvijek always
uz + acc beside
uzimati to take

uzletjeti (uzletim) to take off (plane)
uznemiravati to disturb
uznemiren upset
uzvratiti poziv to call back

vadičep corkscrew
val wave
valna dužina channel
valuta currency
vani outside
vata cotton wool
vatra fire, light (for cigarette)
vatrogasci fire brigade
vatromet firework
važan, važna important
večer evening
večera dinner
večerati to have dinner
već already
većina the majority
vegetarijanac, vegetarijanka vegetarian
velegrad city
veleposlanstvo embassy
veličina size
velik big, great
Velika Britanija Great Britain
velški Welsh
veljača February
vesta sweater
veza connection
vi you
vidjeti (vidim) to see
vijećnica town hall
vijest news item
vijesti news (on radio, TV)
vikend weekend

vila villa
viljuška fork
vino wine
visok high, tall
visoki krvni tlak high blood pressure
više voljeti (volim) to prefer
više more
vitraž stained-glass window
viza visa
vjenčani married
vjerovati (vjerujem) to believe
vješalica za kapute coathanger
vjetar wind
vjetrobran windscreen
vlaga damp
vlak train
vlasnik, vlasnica owner
vlastiti own *(adj)*
voda water; **voda koja nije za piće** non-drinking water
vodič guide, guidebook
vodoinstalater plumber
voljeti (volim) to like, to love
vozačka dozvola driving licence
vozilo hitne pomoći ambulance
voziti to drive
vozni red timetable
vožnja drive *(noun)*
vraćati, vraćati se to give back, to return
vrat neck
vrata door
vratiti se to come back
vrč jug
vreća za spavanje sleeping bag
vremenska prognoza weather forecast
vremenska razlika time difference

vrh summit, top
vrijedi (za) valid (for)
vrijediti to be worth
vrijeme time, weather
vrijeme zatvaranja closing time
vrlo very
vrsta type
vrt garden
vruć hot
vruća čokolada hot chocolate
vrućina heat
vući (vučem) to pull
vuna wool

W

Wales Wales
Walkman Walkman®
WC cloakroom, toilet
WC papir toilet paper
web stranica website
whisky scotch *(whisky)*

Z

za + *acc* for
zabava party
zabavište funfair
zabranjen forbidden
zabraviti to lock
začin spice
zadovoljan, zadovoljna pleased
zadovoljstvo pleasure
zaglavljen stuck
zahvaljivati (zahvaljujem) to thank
zajedno together
zalazak sunca sunset
zamalo almost
zamrzivač freezer

zanimanje profession
zaokret unazad U-turn
zapad west
zaporka za vrata door code
zaposlen busy *(person)*
zarazan, zarazna contagious
zaručnica fiancée
zaručnik fiancé
zastoj delay
zaštititi to protect
zašto why
zatvoren closed
zatvoriti to close
zaustaviti to stop
zauzet engaged
zavoj bandage, dressing
završiti to finish
zbog toga therefore
zbogom goodbye
zdjela bowl
zdravlje health
zelen green
zemlja country, earth
zemljovid map
zglavak wrist
zgodan, zgodna nice, good-
  looking
zgrada building
zima winter
zlatarnica jeweller's
značiti to mean
znak sign
znamenitost landmark
znati to know
znoj sweat
zoološki vrt zoo
zračna luka airport

zrak air
zrakoplov aeroplane
zrakoplovom by airmail
zrcalo mirror
zreo, zrela mature, ripe
zub tooth
zubar dentist
zum zoom (lens)
zvati (zovem) to call
zvono bell, ring
začep: imati začep to be
  constipated

Ž

žaliti se to complain
žaoka sting *(noun)*
žarulja light bulb
žeđ thirst
žedan, žedna thirsty
žena woman
ženski WC ladies' (toilet)
žičara ski lift
žilet razor blade
živ alive
živčan nervous
živjeli! cheers!
živjeti (živim) to live
život life
životinja animal
žlica spoon
žličica teaspoon
žohar cockroach
žuran, žurna urgent
žuriti se to be in a hurry
žurni express
žut yellow

GRAMMAR

There are no **ARTICLES** in Croatian, although the word for the number one (**jedan**) is sometimes used as an indefinite article (a or an).

NOUNS Every word has a gender – masculine *m*, feminine *f* and neuter *n*. Except in some obvious cases (man, woman, father, mother, and so on) these genders have no meaning and must be learned each time you learn a new word. There are, however, some rules:

Most masculine nouns end in a consonant:
>   **brod** boat, **grad** town

Most feminine nouns end in **-a**:
>   **gitara** guitar, **knjiga** book

There are, however, a few feminine nouns which end in a consonant:
>   **noć** night

Most neuter nouns end in **-o** or **-e**:
>   **nebo** sky, **more** sea

The plural of masculine nouns is formed by adding **-i** to the singular or **-ovi** in the case of words of only one syllable:
>   **balkon** balcony, **balkoni** balconies
>   **grad** town, **gradovi** towns

A few masculine nouns have irregular plural forms:
>   **čovjek** man, **ljudi** men

Feminine nouns ending in **-a** change the final letter to **-e** in the plural and the few feminine nouns ending in a consonant add **-i**:
>   **čaša** glass, **čaše** glasses
>   **riječ** word, **riječi** words

In the plural of nearly all neuter nouns the final vowel changes to **-a**:
>   **selo** village, **sela** villages

Nouns, adjectives and pronouns all decline. This means that they have different endings according to the function they have in the sentence. There are seven cases: nominative, genitive, dative, accusative, vocative, instrumental and locative.

The **nominative**, which is the form you will find in dictionaries, is the subject case:

> **autobus** kreće the bus is leaving

The **genitive** expresses belonging and can be called the "of" case:

> čaša **vina** a glass of wine

It is also used after many prepositions, especially those conveying spatial relationships:

> **do** up to; **od** from, away from; **kod** at, at the house of; **blizu** near to; **oko** around
>
> Opatija je kod **Rijeke** Opatija is near Rijeka
>
> ostajemo ovdje do **nedelje** we're staying here until Sunday

The **dative** is the "indirect object" case, indicating the person to whom something is given or spoken. Its form is identical to that of the locative:

> dat ćemo ključ **recepcionaru** we'll give the key to the receptionist

It can also indicate the direction of a movement.

> idemo kući we're going home (to the house)

The **accusative** is the "direct object" case, answering the question "who" or "what" after a transitive verb:

> volim **Dubrovnik** I like Dubrovnik

For masculine inanimate and neuter nouns, the ending is the same as the nominative, but for masculine animate and feminine nouns, it changes:

> volim **jadransku obalu** I like the Adriatic coast
>
> tražim **prijatelja** I'm looking for (my) friend

The **vocative** is used to address someone:

> **gospođo!** Madam!   **gospodine!** Sir!

The **instrumental** is used for the means by which an action is carried out:

> ići ćemo **autobusom** we'll go by bus

The **locative** is always preceded by a preposition. Its main use is to indicate the place where an action occurs:

bili smo u **muzeju** we were in the museum
ostat ćemo na **plaži** we'll stay on the beach

It is also used with the preposition **o** (about):

da li govore o **privatnoj fešti**? are they talking about a private party?

Some consonants change when followed by the feminine locative ending **-i**:
k, **g** and **h** become respectively **c**, **z** and **s** :

knjiga *(nominative)* book u knjizi *(locative)* in the book

The same phenomenon occurs in other situations, for example:
before **-e**: **k**, **g** and **h** become **č**, **ž** and **š**:

friend, companion: **drug** *(nominative)* → druže *(vocative)*

Table of noun declensions

• Masculine nouns

	poklon gift		**student** student	
	singular	*plural*	*singular*	*plural*
nom	poklon	pokloni	student	studenti
gen	poklona	poklona	studenta	studenata
dat	poklonu	poklonima	studentu	studentima
acc	poklon	poklone	studenta	studente
voc	poklone	pokloni	studente	studenti
instr	poklonom	poklonima	studentom	studentima
loc	poklonu	poklonima	studentu	studentima

NB If a masculine noun is inanimate (like **poklon**), the accusative is the same as the nominative and if it is animate (like **student**), the accusative is the same as the genitive.

• Monosyllabic masculine nouns (plural in **-ovi** or **-evi**)

	grad town		**čaj** tea	
	singular	*plural*	*singular*	*plural*
nom	grad	gradovi	čaj	čajevi
gen	grada	gradova	čaja	čajeva
dat	gradu	gradovima	čaju	čajevima
acc	grad	gradove	čaj	čajeve
voc	grade	gradovi	čaj	čajevi

instr	gradom	gradovima	čajem	čajevima
loc	gradu	gradovima	čaju	čajevima

• Neuter nouns ending in -o or -e with the plural ending in -a (the majority)

	more sea		**selo** village	
	singular	*plural*	*singular*	*plural*
nom	more	mora	selo	sela
gen	mora	mora	sela	sela
dat	moru	morima	selu	selima
acc	more	mora	selo	sela
voc	more	mora	selo	sela
instr	morem	morima	selom	selima
loc	moru	morima	selu	selima

• Neuter nouns ending in -e with the plural ending in -na or -ta

	ime nom	
	singular	*plural*
nom	ime	imena
gen	imena	imena
dat	imenu	imenima
acc	ime	imena
voc	ime	imena
instr	imenom	imenima
loc	imenu	imenima

• Feminine nouns ending in -a (the majority)

	žena woman	
	singular	*plural*
nom	žena	žene
gen	žene	žena
dat	ženi	ženama
acc	ženu	žene
voc	ženo	žene
instr	ženom	ženama
loc	ženi	ženama

• Feminine nouns ending in a consonant

obitelj family

	singular	*plural*
nom	obitelj	obitelji
gen	obitelji	obitelji
dat	obitelji	obiteljima
acc	obitelj	obitelji
voc	obitelji	obitelji
instr	obitelji	obiteljima
loc	obitelji	obiteljima

NUMBERS The number one, **jedan, jedna, jedno**, is an adjective, as are all numbers ending in 1 (21, 31, 101, etc). The number and the noun which follows must go into the appropriate case for its function in the sentence:

imam jedan kufer I have one suitcase
jednu kavu, molim one coffee, please
idem s jednim prijateljem I'm going with one friend

Numbers 2, 3, 4 and all numbers finishing in 2, 3 or 4 are followed by the genitive singular:

četiri tanjura four plates
četrdeset i dvije godine forty-two years

The number 2, **dva**, has also a feminine form, **dvije**, and a neuter form, **dvoje**.

Numbers from 5 to 9, including all compounds ending in the numbers 5 to 9, are followed by the genitive plural:

šezdeset devet kuna sixty-nine kunas
pedeset pet minuta fifty-five minutes

Ordinal numbers (see p 120) are adjectives and agree in gender, number and case with the noun that follows them:

	masculine	*feminine*	*neuter*	*m pl*	*f pl*	*n pl*
first	**prvi**	**prva**	**prvo**	**prvi**	**prve**	**prva**

Like nouns, **ADJECTIVES** are declined. They are placed before the noun they describe and agree with it in gender, number and case:

malo dijete a small child
noćni bar a nightclub

mali small

	singular m, f, n	*plural m, f, n*
nom	mali, mala, malo	mali, male, mala
gen	malog, male, malog	malih, malih, malih
dat	malom, maloj, malom	malim, malim, malim
acc	mali/malog, malu, malo	male, male, mala
voc	mali, mala, malo	mali, male, mala
instr	malim, malom, malim	malim, malim, malim
loc	malom, maloj, malom	malim, malim, malim

noćni nocturnal, night

	singular m, f, n	*plural m, f, n*
nom	noćni, noćna, noćno	noćni, noćne, noćna
gen	noćnog, noćne, noćnog	noćnih, noćnih, noćnih
dat	noćnom, noćnoj, noćnom	noćnim, noćnim, noćnim
acc	noćnog, noćnu, noćno	noćne, noćne, noćna
voc	noćni, noćna, noćno	noćni, noćne, noćna
instr	noćnim, noćnom, noćnim	noćnim, noćnim, noćnim
loc	noćnom, noćnoj, noćnom	noćnim, noćnim, noćnim

The **comparative** is generally formed by the additon of the endings **-iji**, **-ji** or **-ši**:

> **nov** new: nov**iji** m, nov**ija** f, nov**ije** n
>
> **jak** strong: ja**či** m, ja**ča** f, ja**če** n (note the change of **k** to **č** when followed by **e**)
>
> **lak** light, easy: lak**ši** m, lak**ša** f, lak**še** n (note the addition of **š**)

The **superlative** is formed by adding the prefix **naj-** to the comparative:

> **nov**: **naj**noviji m, **naj**novija f, **naj**novije n
>
> **jak**: **naj**jači m, **naj**jača f, **naj**jače n
>
> **lak**: **naj**lakši m, **naj**lakša f, **naj**lakše n

PERSONAL PRONOUNS are also declined:

	nom	gen	dat	acc	voc	instr	loc
I	ja	mene	meni	mene	–	(sa) mnom	(o) meni
you	ti	tebe	tebi	tebe	ti	(s) tobom	(o) tebi
he	on	njega	njemu	njega	–	njim	njemu
she	ona	nju	njoj	nju	–	njom	njoj
it	ono	njega	njemu	njega	–	njim	njemu
we	mi	nas	nama	nas	–	nama	nama
you	vi	vas	vama	vas	vi	vama	vama
they	oni	njih	njima	njih	–	njima	njima

NB Personal pronouns are generally omitted when they are the subject of the verb as the person performing the action of the verb is clear from the verb endings. But they must be used in cases other than the nominative, for emphasis and after prepositions.

Possessive prounouns and **possessive adjectives** have the same form:
  moje selo my village
  to je moje that's mine
Like adjectives they agree in gender and case with the noun they are describing or substituting:

nom singular

my, mine	moj *m*, moja *f*, moje *n*
your, yours	tvoj *m*, tvoja *f*, tvoje *n*
his	njegov *m*, njegova *f*, njegovo *n*
her, hers	njen/njezin *m*, njena/njezina *f*, njeno/njezino *n*
our, ours	naš *m*, naša *f*, naše *n*
your, yours	vaš *m*, vaša *f*, vaše *n*
their, theirs	njihov *m*, njihova *f*, njihovo *n*

nom plural

my, mine	moji *m*, moje *f*, moja *n*
your, yours	tvoji *m*, tvoje *f*, tvoja *n*
his	njegovi *m*, njegove *f*, njegova *n*
her, hers	njeni *m*, njene *f*, njena *n*
our, ours	naši *m*, naše *f*, naša *n*
your, yours	vaši *m*, vaše *f*, vaša *n*
their, theirs	njihovi *m*, njihove *f*, njihova *n*

GRAMMAR

VERBS are classified into seven types, according to the first person singular of the present tense:

Infinitives in -ati and first person present in **-am**:

čekati to wait → (ja) čekam I wait, I am waiting

Infinitives in -iti and first person present in **-im**:

raditi to do → (ja) radim I do, I am doing

Infinitives in -eti or -ati and first person present in **-im**:

voljeti to like, to love → (ja) volim I like, I love

držati to hold → (ja) držim I hold, I am holding

Infinitives in -ati and first person present in **-em**:

pisati to write → (ja) pišem I write, I am writing

Infinitives in -ovati or -ivati and first person present in **-ujem**:

putovati to travel → putujem I travel, I am travelling

dosađivati se to be bored → dosađujem se (ja) I'm bored

Infinitives in -nuti and first person present in **-nem**:

brinuti se to be worried → brinem se (ja) I worry, I am worried

Infinitives in a consonant + -ti or in -uti and first person present in **-em** or **-jem**:

pasti to fall → (ja) padnem I fall

čuti to hear → (ja) čujem I hear, I am hearing

The verb **to be** has a long and a short form:

ja sam Dubravka I am Dubravka

jesi li ti Dubravka? – Jesam are you Dubravka? – yes, I am

NB The short form is the norm. The long form is used only when asking questions and answering them as in the exchange above

biti to be

	short form	*long form*
I am	ja **sam**	**jesam**
you are	ti **si**	**jesi**
he/she/it is	on/ona/ono **je**	**jeste**
we are	mi **smo**	**jesmo**
you are	vi **ste**	**jeste**
they are	oni/one/ona **su**	**jesu**

There is also a negative form; the prefix **ni-** is placed in front of the short form:

(ja) **nisam** … I am not …

The verb **to have** also has a negative form:

imati to have

	affirmative form	negative form
I have	(ja) **imam**	**nemam**
you have	(ti) **imaš**	**nemaš**
he/she/it has	(on/ona/ono) **ima**	**nema**
we have	(mi) **imamo**	**nemamo**
you have	(vi) **imate**	**nemate**
they have	(oni/one/ona) **imaju**	**nemaju**

Tenses are less complicated than in English.

In Croatian there is only one form of the present to express both the simple and the continuous present (eg I speak, I am speaking).

The **present** is formed by adding the following endings to the stem vowel: **-a-**, **-e-** or **-i-**:

1st person sg **-m**	1st person pl **-mo**
2nd person sg **-š**	2nd person pl **-te**
3rd person sg **-a**, **-i** or **-e**	3rd person pl **-aju**, **-e** or **-u**

	gledati to look	govoriti to speak	rasti to grow
(ja)	gledam	govorim	rastem
(ti)	gledaš	govoriš	rasteš
(on/ona/ono)	gleda	govori	raste
(mi)	gledamo	govorimo	rastemo
(vi)	gledate	govorite	rastete
(oni/one/ona)	gledaju	govore	rastu

To make a **negative sentence**, **ne** is added before the verb:
  ne govorim hrvatski I don't speak Croatian

To ask **questions**, the interrogative particle **li** is added after the verb:
  govoriš **li** hrvatski? do you speak Croatian?

You may also hear the words **da li** at the beginning of a sentence. This structure is slightly easier to use, but it is more correct to use the verb + **li** structure.

The only **past tense** you need to know is a compound form, using the short form of **biti** followed by the past participle of the verb, derived from the infinitive. This is an adjectival form, which agrees in gender and number with the subject of the verb. The following endings are added to the stem:

-o *(m sg)*, -la *(f sg)*, -lo *(n sg)*, -li *(m pl)*, -le *(f pl)*, -la *(n pl)*

The negative is formed by using the negative form of **biti** followed by the participle:

(ja) nisam razumio *m*; (ja) nisam razumjela *f* I didn't understand

govoriti to speak
If the subject is masculine:

affirmative	*negative*
ja **sam** govorio	ja **ni**sam govorio
ti **si** govorio	ti **ni**si govorio
on **je** govorio	on **ni**je govorio
mi **smo** govorili	mi **ni**smo govorili
vi **ste** govorili	vi **ni**ste govorili
oni **su** govorili	oni **ni**su govorili

If the subject is feminine :

affirmative	*negative*
ja **sam** govorila	ja **ni**sam govorila
tl **sl** govorlla	tl **nl**sl govorlla
ona **je** govorila	ona **ni**je govorila
mi **smo** govorile	mi **ni**smo govorile
vi **ste** govorile	vi **ni**ste govorile
one **su** govorile	one **ni**su govorile

The future is formed by combining the infinitive with the auxiliary verb **htjeti** (to want). Like biti, **htjeti** has two forms:

	short form	*long form*
I want/shall	(ja) **ću**	(ja) **hoću**
you want/will	(ti) **ćeš**	(ti) **hoćeš**
he/she wants/will	(on/ona/ono) **će**	(on/ona/ono) **hoće**
we want/shall	(mi) **ćemo**	(mi) **hoćemo**
you want/will	(vi) **ćete**	(vi) **hoćete**
they want/will	(oni/one/ona) **će**	(oni/one/ona) **hoće**

There is also a negative form, formed in the same way as the negative form of biti: by adding ne- to the short form, this time of htjeti. So, for instance "I shall speak" will be ja ću govoriti, while "I shan't speak" is: ja neću govoriti, etc.

affirmative	*negative*
ja ću govoriti	ja neću govoriti
ti ćeš govoriti	ti nećeš govoriti
on/ona/ono će govoriti	on/ona/ono neće govoriti
mi ćemo govoriti	mi nećemo govoriti
vi ćete govoriti	vi nećete govoriti
oni/one/ona će govoriti	oni/one/ona neće govoriti

The long form is used when asking questions and answering them with a one-word answer:

hoću li (ja) govoriti?	**hoću**
hoćeš li (ti) govoriti?	**hoćeš**
hoće li (on/ona/ono) govoriti?	**hoće**
hoćemo li (mi) govoriti?	**hoćemo**
hoćete li (vi) govoriti?	**hoćete**
hoće li (oni/one/ona) govoriti?	**hoće**

NB In Croatian it is normal to answer a question with a verb, rather than either da yes or ne no.

If the personal pronoun is not used, the auxiliary is placed after the infinitive. If the verb ends in -ti (eg **govoriti** to speak), the final i is omitted. If the infinitive ends in -ći (eg **ići** to go), it is written in full:

govoriti		**ići**	
govorit ću	govorit ćemo	ići ću	ići ćemo
govorit ćeš	govorit ćete	ići ćeš	ići ćete
govorit će	govorit će	ići će	ići će

HOLIDAYS AND FESTIVALS

NATIONAL BANK HOLIDAYS

1 January	**Nova godina** New Year
6 January	**Sveta tri kralja** Epiphany
March/April	**Uskršnji ponedjeljak** Easter Monday
1 May	**Praznik rada** May Day/Labour Day
10 June	**Tijelovo** Corpus Christi
22 June	**Dan antifašističke borbe** Antifascist Resistance Day
25 June	**Dan državnosti** National Day
5 August	**Dan pobjede i domovinske zahvalnosti** Victory and Thanksgiving Day
15th August	**Velika gospa** Assumption
8th October	**Dan neovisnosti** Independence Day
1st November	**Svi sveti** All Saints
25th, 26th December	**Božićni blagdani** Christmas and Boxing Day

FESTIVALS AND CELEBRATIONS

January–March	**Riječki karneval** (Rijeka Carnival)
3 February	**Fešta Svetog Vlaha** (Feast of St Vlaho, the patron saint of Dubrovnik)
April	**Music Biennale Zagreb** (Festival of Contemporary Music)
June–July	**Međunarodni dječji festival u Šibeniku** (Šibenik Children's Festival)
July	**Međunarodna smotra folklora** (International Festival of Folklore, Zagreb: an opportunity to discover the traditional music of south-east Europe)
July	**Splitsko ljeto** (Split Festival: opera, theatre, ballet, concerts)
July	**Festival dalmatinskih klapa Omiš** (Festival of Dalmatian polyphonic songs in Omiš)

uly	**Pulski filmski festival** (Pula Film Festival)
uly–August	**Zagrebački barokni festival** (Zagreb Baroque Festival)
uly–August	**Dubrovačke ljetne igre** (Dubrovnik Summer Festival: an arts festival of international renown, featuring theatre, classical music, folk dancing, exhibitions of fine art, literature and midnight serenades)
early August	**Sinjska alka** (Sinj Tournament: chivalric games dating from 1715 in which participants must thrust lances through the Ring of Sinj at full gallop)
Sept–Oct	**Varaždinske barokne večeri** (Varaždin Baroque Evenings)

USEFUL ADDRESSES

Before you set off, you can get plenty of useful information from the following organizations:

In the UK

Croatian National Tourist Office, UK
2 The Lanchesters, 162–164 Fulham Palace Road, London W6 9ER
Tel: 020 8563 7979
Fax: 020 8563 2616
E-mail: info@cnto.freeserve.co.uk

British Embassy, Zagreb
Vlaška 121/III Floor PO Box 454 10000 Zagreb
Tel: (00 385) 1 455 5310
Fax: (00 385) 1 455 1685
E-mail: british-embassy@zg.tel.hr

British Consulate, Split
Obala hrvatskog narodnog preporoda 10/III 21000 Split
Tel: (00 385) 21 341 464
Fax: (00 385) 21 362 905

British Consulate, Dubrovnik
Atlas Pile 1 20000 Dubrovnik
Tel: (00 385) 20 412 916
Fax: (00 385) 20 412 916

Croatian Embassy, London
21 Conway Street, London W1P 5HL
Tel: 020 7387 2022
Fax: 020 7387 0310

In the US

Croatian National Tourist Office, USA
350 Fifth Avenue, Suite 4003, New York 10118, USA
Tel: (00 1) 212 279 8672
Fax: (00 1) 212 279 8683
E-mail: cntony@earthlink.net

US Embassy, Zagreb
Tel: (00 385) 1 455 5500
Fax: (00 385) 1 455 8585
Website: www.usembassy.hr

Croatian Embassy, Washington DC
2343 Massachusetts Ave, NW Washington, DC 20008 USA
Tel: (00 1) 202-588-8497
Fax: (00 1) 202-234-2363

Emergency phone numbers in Croatia

Directory enquiries: 988 (national), 902 (international)
Police: 92
Fire brigade: 93
Medical emergencies: 94
Breakdown: 987
Sea rescue: 9155

CONVERSION TABLES

Note that when writing numbers, Croatian uses a comma where English uses a full stop. For example 0.6 would be written 0,6 in Croatian.

MEASUREMENTS

Only the metric system is used in Croatia.

Length   Distance

1 cm ≈ 0.4 inches	1 metre ≈ 1 yard
30 cm ≈ 1 foot	1 km ≈ 0.6 miles

To convert kilometres into miles, divide by 8 and then multiply by 5.

kilometres	1	2	5	10	20	100
miles	0.6	1.25	3.1	6.25	12.50	62.50

To convert miles into kilometres, divide by 5 and then multiply by 8.

miles	1	2	5	10	20	100
kilometres	1.6	3.2	8	16	32	160

Weight

25g ≈ 1 oz   1 kg ≈ 2 lb   6 kg ≈ 1 stone

To convert kilos into pounds, divide by 5 and then multiply by 11.
To convert pounds into kilos, multiply by 5 and then divide by 11.

kilos	1	2	10	20	60	80
pounds	2.2	4.4	22	44	132	176

Liquid

1 litre ≈ 2 pints
4.5 litres ≈ 1 gallon

Temperature

To convert temperatures in Fahrenheit into Celsius, subtract 32, multiply by 5 and then divide by 9.

To convert temperatures in Celsius into Fahrenheit, divide by 5, multiply by 9 and then add 32.

Fahrenheit (°F)	32	40	50	59	68	86	100
Celsius (°C)	0	4	10	15	20	30	38

Clothes sizes

Sometimes you will find sizes given using the English-language abbreviations **XS** (Extra Small), **S** (Small), **M** (Medium), **L** (Large) and **XL** (Extra Large).

• Women's clothes

Europe	36	38	40	42	44	etc
UK	8	10	12	14	16	

• Bras (cup sizes are the same)

Europe	70	75	80	85	90	etc
UK	32	34	36	38	40	

• Men's shirts (collar size)

Europe	36	38	41	43	etc
UK	14	15	16	17	

• Men's clothes

Europe	40	42	44	46	48	50	etc
UK	30	32	34	36	38	40	

Shoe sizes

• Women's shoes

Europe	37	38	39	40	42	etc
UK	4	5	6	7	8	

• Men's shoes

Europe	40	42	43	44	46	etc
UK	7	8	9	10	11	